How to Judge People by What They Look Like

Edward Dutton

Thomas Edward Press

Table of Contents

About the Author

Edward Dutton is a freelance researcher and writer. Born in London in 1980, he lives in Finland and is Adjunct Professor of the Anthropology of Religion at Oulu University. Dutton was educated at Durham University, where he graduated in Theology in 2002, and Aberdeen University, from which he received his PhD in Religious Studies in 2006.

Dutton has been guest researcher at Leiden University in the Netherlands and Umeå University in Sweden, and has been academic consultant at King Saud University in Saudi Arabia. He has published widely in psychology in such journals as *Intelligence, Personality and Individual Differences* and *Evolutionary Psychological Science.* Dutton's other books include: *Meeting Jesus at University: Rites of Passage and Student Evangelicals* (Routledge, 2016), *Religion and Intelligence: An Evolutionary Analysis* (Ulster Institute for Social Research, 2014) and *The Genius Famine* (University of Buckingham Press, 2015) (jointly with Bruce Charlton). Dutton's research has been reported in newspapers worldwide. In his spare time, Dutton enjoys genealogy and has written many articles on the subject. He is married to a Finnish Lutheran priest and has two children. He can be found online at www.edwarddutton.wordpress.com

Acknowledgements

I would like to thank Prof. Dimitri Van der Linden, Prof. Guy Madison and Dr Bruce Charlton for their helpful comments on earlier drafts of this short book.

Foreword by Prof Bruce Charlton

Appearances are not always deceptive. Indeed, quite the opposite. In this highly informative and entertaining mini-book, Dr Dutton surveys the psychological data in support of the neglected idea that we can tell a lot about someone from how they look. The fact that most people believe they can judge a stranger by their face and body makes it plausible that we really can do this, if not with total accuracy, then at least to a useful degree. It is a question of probabilities. So long as we are better than random at predicting traits such as personality, intelligence or aggression; overall this would have a positive impact on reproductive success. As social mammals, this attribute would have been very helpful, and sometimes vital, during our evolutionary history. Dr Dutton's book is a necessary corrective to misleading modern myths and taboos about 'judgmentalism' and stereotyping. As he makes clear; so long as we are prepared to modify our first impressions in the light of further evidence; it is reasonable and sensible to take seriously our innate ability to sum-up a stranger with a glance.

Prof. Bruce Charlton
Reader in Evolutionary Psychiatry at Newcastle University and Visiting Professor of Theoretical Medicine at the University of Buckingham.

Chapter One

The Strange Death of Physiognomy

'People say sometimes that Beauty is only superficial. That may be so. But at least it is not so superficial as Thought. To me, Beauty is the wonder of wonders. It is only shallow people who do not judge by appearances.' Oscar Wilde, *The Picture of Dorian Gray.*

Everyone's heard the cliché, 'Don't judge a book by its cover.' Don't judge people by their appearance. Judge people, if you have to judge them at all, by what's in their hearts. It's a warm, cuddly idea: that nobody can help what they look like and what they look like is nothing to do with what they actually *are* like. Imploring people not to judge by appearances has many benefits: it makes you seem kind, for one, and it emphasises your profundity. You are somehow able to rise above your instincts, ignore the 'superficial,' and plunge into the depths of people's hearts.

In the 2001 comedy *Shallow Hal,* Jack Black plays Hal Larsen, who is obsessed with physical beauty. Hal's superficiality appals the 'life success coach' Tony Robbins (who plays himself). Robbins ends up sharing an elevator with Hal. Robbins hypnotises Hal such that he can only see people's inner beauty. If they're a good person then they'll be attractive; if they're a nasty person then they'll look hideous. Accordingly, Hal ends-up dating an extremely kind but morbidly obese young woman, played by Gwyneth Paltrow. Unaccountably, from Hal's perspective, chairs collapse under this slender goddess, she creates an enormous splash at the local swimming pool, and she has a bizarrely negative opinion of her own appearance. Most of us would like to think that we are like the hypnotized Hal and that we 'Don't judge a book by its cover.'

1. The Wisdom of the Ancients

Except, we generally do. Despite gaining all the social benefits of claiming we don't judge by appearances we almost certainly do so, even if only unconsciously. And we do so because we are evolved to do so, and because doing so has worked up until now. Oscar Wilde (1854-1900) quipped, in *The Picture of Dorian Gray,* 'Only shallow people do not judge by appearances' (Wilde, 2012). In Medieval and

Early Modern England, it went without saying that you judged by appearances. Although the hypotheses which underpinned their thought-systems – such as astrology – were hopeless, our ancestors had it partly right when it came to what is called 'physiognomy.' This is the attempt to judge a person's character from what they look like.

The Ancient Greeks were firm believers in physiognomy. Aristotle (384-322 BC) wrote in *Prior Analytics* that, 'It is possible to infer character from features' (Aristotle, 1989) and many other Greek scholars took the same view. Michael Scot (1175-1232), a Scottish mathematician and a scholar at the court of the Holy Roman Emperor, wrote a learned thesis on the subject (Porter, 2005, p.122). In the late 14th century work *Canterbury Tales,* the author, Geoffrey Chaucer (c.1343-1400), gives the Wife of Bath a gap in her front teeth to imply that she is highly sexual. The Reeve is of slim build, to suggest he is 'choleric' (bad-tempered and irritable), while the Summoner is ugly, because he's an unpleasant person (see Hallissy, 1995). Physiognomy was taught as an academic subject at English universities, until it was outlawed by Henry VIII (r.1509-1547) for having become associated with fortune-telling (Porter, 2005, p.134).

Even so, it continued to be widely accepted in academic and literary circles. Shakespeare made frequent use of it (see Baumbach, 2008). This is most obvious in Julius Caesar's description of Cassius:

> 'Let me have men about me that are fat
> Sleek-headed men and such as sleep a-nights
> Yond Cassius has a lean and hungry look
> He thinks too much. Such men are dangerous'
> (*Julius Caesar,* Act I, Scene II).

The medic Thomas Browne (1605-1682) published his *Religio Medici* in 1643, in which he observed, 'there is surely a Physiognomy, which those experienced and Master Mendicants observe . . . For there are mystically in our faces certain Characters that carry in them the motto of our Souls, wherein he that cannot read A.B.C. may read our natures' (Browne, 1844, p.102).

Physiognomy fell into disrepute precisely because of its association with 'Master Mendicants,' but it was then re-popularised by the Swiss scholar Johan Kaspar Lavater (1741-1801) (see Lavater, 1826). Up until Lavater, people had believed that there were a number of 'general types' of people, with physiognomy allowing you to discern which type a person was: *choleric* (temperamental), *phlegmatic* (calm), *mercurial* (changeable and unpredictable) or *sanguine* (optimistic). Lavater developed this, arguing that physiognomy could be used to be far more specific – to discern the character traits of individuals. Physiognomy was duly revived and by the nineteenth century it was implicit in many novels, and most obviously in *The Picture of Dorian Gray,* which was written in 1890. Dorian wants to maintain his beauty but live an amoral and hedonistic life. Accordingly, he sells his soul in return for his amoral life being reflected in a portrait of him, rather than on his own face and body. He remains beautiful, while the portrait becomes increasingly unattractive. In many other Victorian novels, besides, the good characters were physically attractive while the bad characters were ugly and deformed. Appearance was, once again, a short-hand for character (see essays in Percival & Tytler, 2005). Famously, the captain of *The Beagle,* Robert Fitzroy, wanted an 'energetic young man' as a gentleman companion on his voyage. The nature of Charles Darwin's nose told Fitzroy that Darwin could not possibly be that man. Darwin's daughter, Henrietta, later stated that Fitzroy had 'made up his mind that no man with such a nose could have energy.' Fortunately, the rest of Darwin's face compensated for this: 'His brow saved him' (quoted in Highfield et al., 2009).

And this is where the English gentleman scientist Sir Francis Galton (1822-1911) makes an appearance. Statistician, polymath, social scientist, proto-geneticist, inventor, meteorologist, geographer and even tropical explorer, Galton was Renaissance man. If there was a belief that remained yet to be scientifically proved or disproved, Galton was drawn to proving or disproving it (see Bulmer, 2004). Physiognomy, therefore, fascinated him. In 1878, Galton published an article in the journal *Nature* in which he presented his findings. He developed a system of composite photographs in which he superimposed a variety of faces onto each other using multiple exposures. This allowed him to create photographic representations of those with certain qualities, such as being beautiful, criminal or ill. These led to distinct photographs, implying, for example, that there is a degree to which criminals have distinct faces from the rest of the population.

Unfortunately, physiognomy became associated – and, perhaps, remains associated – with phrenology. Pioneered by

German scientist Franz Josef Gall (1758-1828), this was the belief that the nature of a person's character can be discerned by small differences in the shape of their skull. As the brain is an organ, and different parts of the brain have different functions, it seemed to follow that bumps or indentations in the skull would reflect similar properties in the brain. As such, people could 'have their lumps felt' and it would reveal a great deal about the nature of their personality; albeit based on the very limited nineteenth century knowledge of brain modules. Phrenology became hugely popular in the late eighteenth and early nineteenth centuries, with the establishment of learned phrenology societies, including a significant one in Edinburgh (see de Giustino, 2016). The Edinburgh Phrenological Society was founded by the Scottish solicitor George Combe (1788-1858) who asserted, 'that the brain is the organ of mind; that the brain is an aggregate of several parts, each subserving a distinct mental faculty; and that the size of the cerebral organ is, caeteris paribus, an index of power or energy of function' (quoted in Fodor, 1983, p.131). Unsurprisingly, phrenology was debunked. Physiognomy found itself (intellectually) guilty by association.

2. 'Not by the colour of their skin . . .'

The other problem physiognomy has to deal with is the obvious unpleasant consequences judging people by their appearance has when it comes to the issue of 'race.' This is most obvious in the case of a bunch of nasty, anti-intellectuals who took power in Germany and attempted to wipe out the race which they regarded as their own race's chief competitor. The Nazis measured facial features in order to determine the archetypal 'Jew' and the archetypal 'Aryan,' giving the measurement of facial features for any broader purpose a bad name. But the actions of the Nazis are entirely irrelevant. As we will see shortly, physiognomy works, in most cases, within races. We will look more at 'race,' and its relationship with physiognomy, shortly.

But most importantly, if we accept Darwinian Theory, we really must ask ourselves, 'Why wouldn't physiognomy work?' Humans are an advanced form of ape, very closely related to all mammals, such as the lion. Female lions are more attracted to males with darker manes. This is because these males have higher levels of testosterone, as reflected in the colour of their manes, and are thus more aggressive and more likely to win fights. Physiognomy works with lions (West & Packer, 2002). It would be extraordinary if it *didn't* work with humans.

But before proving that it does work, we should be clear on our key terms. I have already defined these terms in detail in my book *The Genius Famine* (Dutton & Charlton, 2015). So those who have read that book may wish to skip this section as much of it is exactly the same as in *The Genius Famine.*

3. Intelligence

It is 'intelligence' and personality that 'physiognomy' tries to discern from what people look like. But how do we define these words? Intelligence refers to the ability to solve cognitive problems quickly. The more intelligent you are the quicker you can solve the problem, and the harder it has to be before you must give up.

Intelligence is measured by IQ tests. IQ test scores in childhood will predict many important things – higher intelligence predicts higher education level, higher socio-economic status, higher salary, better health, greater civic participation, lower impulsivity, a more trusting nature, higher emotional intelligence, and longer lifespan; lower intelligence predicts higher criminality, and shorter-term future-orientation (see Jensen, 1998). Some people argue for a broader or multiple definition of intelligence. In particular, they promote the concept of 'emotional intelligence.' But there is no need to separate this from 'intelligence' as I have defined it here. The ability to solve social problems – such as conflicts between people - has been shown to be predicted by intelligence at 0.3 (Kaufman et al., 2011), a finding which as 'statistically significant.' 'Significance,' it should be noted, in used is science to mean that based on the sample size the relationship between two variables – such as 'intelligence' and 'solving social problems' – is not a fluke. A 'correlation' refers to a relationship between two variables; the extent to which one predicts the other. A 'correlation' of 1 means they perfectly predict each other, a correlation of 0.1 means they only weakly do so, and a correlation of -0.9 means they very strongly negatively predict each other; this is a 'negative correlation.' The correlation is deemed 'statistically significant' if we can be at least 95% certain that it is not a fluke. Only if the correlation is 'statistically significant' do scientists accept that it is real.

Intelligence is measured by IQ (Intelligence Quotient) tests. These measure three forms of intelligence: verbal, numerical (mathematical) and spatial (geometric). Some individuals are higher in one form of intelligence than another, and rarely they may have above average measures in one measure of intelligence and below average in another – but, overall, in group studies all of the many different measures of cognitive ability will always positively correlate. It is consistently found that, within-groups and between-groups, high ability in one task goes hand-in-hand with high ability in other tasks. The positive correlation between these measures means that we can talk about a 'general factor' that underpins all of them. This underlying factor is known as '*g*' for 'general intelligence' (see Jensen, 1998).

Intelligence increases throughout childhood and decreases from middle-age onwards. As such, IQ is a comparative measure – comparing the individual with a group sample of the same age. The IQ number is a way of expressing the individual's position in an ordering of IQ test scores for his age group. The average IQ is 100, often compared to the UK population average. Larger numbers are above the average intelligence and lower numbers are below average. This is expressed in percentage terms based on a so-called normal distribution curve with a standard deviation of 15 IQ points. So, an IQ above 120 is approximately in the top 10% of the population; and 130 in the top 2%.

The results of IQ tests strongly correlate with other measures of thinking ability, such as school work, where the correlation is about 0.7 (Jensen, 1998) and they are not merely culturally influenced (see Jensen, 1998). We know that IQ testing is valid and robust across cultures, because the cultures (or sub-cultures) that score poorly in IQ tests do the least-poorly on the *most* culturally-biased parts of the test, and also because the IQ test results correlate positively with something objective – that is, with differences in simple reaction times – how quickly you hit a switch when a light turns on (Jensen, 1998). The positive correlation between intelligence and reaction times means intelligence is a good indicator of how well the nervous system is running.

As already noted, intelligence is a vital predictor of life outcomes. IQ correlates with school achievement at 0.7, length of time spent in education and undergraduate performance at 0.5, postgraduate performance at 0.4 and salary at 0.3. It is also a clear predictor of job status (Jensen, 1998). It has been found that less-selective professionals, like teachers and nurses, have an IQ of about 110, while it is 120 for doctors and lawyers, and even higher for those who rise to the top of these professions (see Herrnstein & Murray, 1994). Within academia, the average PhD student in education has an IQ of around 117, while the average PhD student in Physics has an IQ of 130 (Harmon, 1961).

Intelligence is around 80% genetic. Overwhelmingly, therefore, intelligence is inherited from your parents (see Lynn, 2011, p.101). Environmental factors include sufficient nutrition and a sufficiently intellectually stimulating environment when growing up. Just as important is an intellectually stimulating adult environment, which those with high intelligence will tend to create for themselves. For this reason, among others, the genetic component of IQ during childhood is relatively low, as the child's environment will reflect its parents' intelligence. Only as the child reaches adulthood will its environment reflect its own intelligence, leading to a genetic component of 80% (see Lynn, 2011).

4. Personality

Personality is, in essence, 'our general way of being.' Differences in personality predict differences in how people will respond in a certain situation. Personality evaluations are usually measured by questionnaires: How close to you does a car moving at a certain speed have to be before you judge that it is too dangerous to cross the road in front of it? How many annoying things have to happen to you in a day before you lose your temper and raise your voice? How strongly do the emotions of others impact how you feel?

Different people will give different answers to these questions, in part because of variation in their personality. Typically, people are asked whether a certain behaviour, or like or dislike, is present or absent in them; or else asked to rate its strength. Multiple such questions can be analysed and averaged to yield a few personality 'traits' which cluster together. The exact number of these traits used by psychologists depends on the purpose of the personality evaluation. The number can be as few as one general master trait (e.g. pro-social versus asocial), or dozens of specific traits such as aggression, or courage – but usually, for convenience, the number of traits used for describing personality have been between about two and five.

Many psychologists currently suggest that personality can best be understood in terms of five essential personality characteristics: these are the 'Big 5':

(1) *Extraversion-Introversion*. Extraversion is a need for external stimulation – especially social stimulation. It involves feeling positive feelings strongly. Introversion is sufficient internal stimulation and, therefore, independence from external stimuli.

(2) *Neuroticism-Emotional Stability*. Neuroticism relates to emotional instability – especially negative mood swings such as anxiety, depression, and shyness.

(3) *Conscientiousness-Impulsiveness*: Conscientiousness refers to responsiveness to social norms, usually leading to organized, rule-following, and self-disciplined behaviour. In essence, it is impulse control.

(4) *Agreeableness-Indifference to other people*: Agreeableness shows itself in a high interest in other people, what they are thinking and how they feel. In other words, it is altruism.

(5) *Openness-Intellect-Aversion to change*: Openness references intellectual curiosity and a preference for novelty, creativity (in some sense of the word), hypnotisability and unusual psychological experiences. Openness weakly but significantly (0.3) correlates with intelligence, as it is measuring some of the same things.

These five personality traits are (except for Openness--Intellect) regarded as independent of IQ scores (at least within normal IQ ranges); and our placing on them predicts how we behave. For example, high Conscientiousness as a child predicts greater success in education and employment; high Neuroticism predicts problems with mood swings, anxiety and depression. High Openness-Intellect will tend to result in being a novelty-loving, impractical, perhaps artistic, academic or spiritual dreamer. A moderately high score, however, is a predictor of artistic success – or at least, on some measures of artistic success that focus on the production of novelty (see Nettle, 2007). Personality traits are between 50% (Nettle, 2007) and 70% genetic (Lynn, 2011).

The Big Five were developed from the Big Three traits defined by psychologist Hans Eysenck (1916-1997), who arrived in England from Germany in the 1930s and became the most important personality in British academic psychology. The Big Three are Extraversion, Neuroticism and Psychoticism. In effect, the Big Five dimensions of Conscientiousness and Agreeableness are the opposites of various aspects of Eysenck's Psychoticism; and Openness takes some aspects of Psychoticism and blends them with behaviours characteristic of modern intellectuals (see Eysenck, 1993). As an aside, Eysenck actually defended a popular Medieval system of thought. He argued that, according to the available data, there was something in astrology. At the very least, people born under particular star signs were more likely to have the personality associated with that star sign than would be predicted by chance (Eysenck, 1997, Ch. 7).

Many scholars have shown that the Big Five (and Big Three) are all co-correlated, and could all therefore be collapsed into a single personality variable, which he called the *General Factor of Personality* (GFP) (e.g. Van der Linden et al., 2016; Rushton & Irwing, 2008). GFP can be conceptualized as the single dimension of personality – from pro-social to a-social – which underlies the more specific personality traits – analogously to how general intelligence or 'g' underlies all the specific cognitive abilities.

So the General Factor of Personality can be conceptualized as the degree to which a personality is pro-social– in other words, the degree to which someone has the kind of personality type and behaviours that underpin many socially desirable traits, the degree to which someone approximates to the type of person that makes for friendliness, helpfulness, being a 'good neighbour'. The GFP describes a basic personality dimension, high levels of which may have evolved as an adaptation in complex and stable societies so that people would 'get along well together'. So a person with high GFP would be sociable, extraverted, concerned with the feelings of others, and self-disciplined in pursuit of socially-approved goals. He'd also have stable emotions, and be open to new ideas (see Rushton & Irwing, 2008).

5. Race and Physiognomy

Finally, we need to understand what 'race' is, because a number of physical traits allow predictions about psychology to be made within races but not between them. It is assumed that the reader is reasonably intelligent. So, I assume there's been no emotional reaction to discussing this 'controversial' topic and we can pursue it in an entirely logical way.

'Race' is employed to refer to what in the animal world would be a subspecies: a breeding population separated from another of the same species long enough to be noticeably evolved to a different environment but not long enough to be unable to have fertile offspring with the other group. In other words, a race is a breeding population that differs genetically from other such populations as a result of geographical isolation, cultural separation, and endogamy, and which shows patterns of genotypic frequency for a number of inter-correlated characteristics compared with other breeding populations. The most obvious manifestations of this are observable differences in physical appearance (see Dutton & Lynn, 2015). It has been clearly demonstrated that humans fall into clear genetic clusters which parallel the 'races' of traditional anthropology (see Jensen, 1998). So, it is quite clear that 'race' is a biological reality and not some kind of 'social construct.'

One criticism of 'race' is that there are more differences within races than there are between them. Likewise, you could argue that there are more differences within humanity and chimpanzees than there are between individual humans and chimpanzees. There is, after all, only a 1.5% genetic difference between humans and chimpanzees (Caccone & Powell, 1989). I don't think many people would argue that the distinction between humans and chimpanzees is meaningless. We are talking about comparative differences. Dividing between two racial categories, for example, permits accurate predictions to be made about each, even if the differences are small. The genetic differences (in terms of heritable musical ability) between a standard musician and Mozart are probably quite small but these differences have crucial consequences. Miniscule genetic differences (humans only differ by 0.0012%) can have significant consequences.

In addition, as Cochran and Harpending (2009, p.15) have noted, there are more genetic differences within breeds of dog than between breeds of dog, but nobody would dismiss as insignificant the differences between a Great Dane and Chihuahua. Further, they note that 'information about the distribution of genetic variation tells you essentially nothing about the size or significance of trait differences . . . If between-group genetic differences tend to push in a particular direction – tend to favour a certain trend – they can add up and have large effects' (see Dutton and Lynn, 2015, for a more detailed discussion of 'race', upon which this section draws).

Rushton (2000) has shown that if we compare the 'Big 3' races – blacks, whites and Northeast Asians – there are clear and consistent differences, with East Asians at one end of spectrum and black people at the other. As these differences already show up in childhood, stand robust against environmental interventions, and as personality is at least 50% genetic and intelligence about 80% so, they are genetic differences. Northeast Asians score the highest in intelligence tests (105), blacks score the lowest (85), while whites are intermediate (100) but closer to Northeast Asians. Within these tests, whites have better verbal intelligence than Northeast Asians but much worse mathematical intelligence, meaning that Northeast Asians come out with higher 'general intelligence' overall. Real predictions about 'character' can be made from this, as intelligence is associated with emotional intelligence, cooperativeness, low self-esteem, a trusting nature, future-orientation, law-abidingness, intellectual curiosity, creativity, leadership ability, having a sense of humour, having a good memory, and even talking speed (see Jensen, 1998).

Furthermore, Rushton (2000) showed that there are race differences in personality traits, in much the same way. Northeast Asians are highest in Agreeableness, black people are lowest and whites are intermediate but closer to Northeast Asians. Black people are highest in Extraversion, Northeast Asians are lowest and whites are intermediate but closer to Northeast Asians. Northeast Asians are the highest in Conscientiousness while black people are the lowest, and the same is true of Neuroticism.

According to the Life History Model of human development, we either invest energy in reproduction or in growth. Investing more energy in reproduction is an r-strategy whereas investing more energy in growth (including nurturing our offspring and competing with other members of our society) is a K strategy. All of us sit somewhere on the r-K continuum. An extreme r-strategy would be for a man to copulate with as many attractive (and thus healthy) and young (and thus fertile) women as possible and invest nothing in the offspring. This so-called 'fast life history strategy' develops in an unstable ecology where you cannot predict anything with much accuracy so you live fast and die young. As the ecology becomes more stable, it reaches its carrying capacity for a particular species. As such, its members start competing against each other and they do this by investing more resources in their offspring, so that their offspring can learn to survive. This predictable yet harsh environment selects for intelligence and impulse control. Rushton argues that the r-K continuum underpins race differences in psychology. Blacks are the most r-strategist because their ecology is subject to unpredictable outbreaks of tropical diseases and has invariant warm weather, meaning basic needs are met. The environment of Northeast Asians is harsh but it is highly predictable.

Clearly, this means you can make very rough judgements about cognitive ability and personality from (racial) appearance. But if you concluded from this that, 'All blacks are stupid' you'd have to be quite fantastically stupid yourself. And if you were Japanese, it'd be very silly to react to this by saying, 'Ha, ha! So we're the best!' Not only are these value judgements irrelevant, they are plain wrong. All we have found is that there are three races each with three bell curves, wherein the average is different. For example, the average IQ of Northeast Asian Americans is 105, for white Americans it is 100 and for black Americans it is 85. In practice, this means that you are unlikely to find many black Americans with IQs of 150 and you are unlikely to find many Japanese Americans with IQs of 50. But there are all kinds of variation in between. This really cannot be stressed enough.

In much the same way, university graduates are, on average, more intelligent than non-graduates. You are unlikely, therefore, to find people with extremely low IQs at university. But there are all kinds of factors other than intelligence which influence whether you go to university: personality, luck, or (sadly) just having rich parents who can afford to send you to a very good school. For this reason, anyone who has attended even a prestigious British university will testify to the presence of some profoundly stupid people. Indeed, there are massive variations in average IQ by subject. The average PhD student in Physics has an IQ of about 130, while the average PhD student in education has an IQ of 117 (Harmon, 1961). This is a difference of almost 15 points, the difference between the average school teacher and the average policeman (Herrnstein & Murray, 1994).

What this all means – in practical terms – is that, if you are particularly paranoid and you are Northeast Asian, it might be worth shunning white people like me. However, this would likely be a very bad strategy to follow because though, by doing so, you will avoid some very dangerous people, you will also fail to interact with many people who could make fantastic colleagues, friends, and even partners.

6. Gender and Age

The same thing is true of gender. On average and in all cultures, females (compared to males) are higher in Extraversion, Neuroticism, Conscientiousness, and Agreeableness. They are higher in the aesthetic aspect of Openness-Intellect but they are lower in 'Intellect' (see Weisberg et al., 2011). As adults (though not as children) females seem to score very slightly lower on IQ tests than men, they have worse spatial and mathematical intelligence but better verbal intelligence, and they have a narrower intelligence range (see Irwing, 2013). This means there are more very stupid males, but also more super-intelligent males, which is likely why most scientific geniuses have been male (see Dutton & Charlton, 2015).

Equally, age is a good marker of intelligence and personality. People reach their intelligence peak in early middle age (see Kirasic, 1989). Throughout life they also become more Conscientious, less Neurotic, and more Agreeable (apart from a dip during their teens) (Soto et al., 2011). Clearly, age can be reasonably well inferred from appearance, though there is obviously significant variation in how quickly people physically (and mentally) age.

7. Beyond the Trickle Effect

But let's go for a subtler approach than race and sex and age. Let's look within these categories. We can look for physical markers – or, better still, collections of physical markers that move in the same direction – which imply certain psychological traits across all races. From a practical perspective, we are social animals and we spend our lives dealing with other people. We want to establish, as quickly as we can, what kind of people they are; especially in risky situations where a correct decision must be made and made quickly. To put it in black and white terms, 'Are they a goodie or a baddie? Do we want to interact with them or not? And if we do want to interact with them, how cautious do we need to be?'

There are sociological ways we can do this, of course, but these are subject to rapid change and so require you to have your finger on the pulse of fashion. The German sociologist Georg Simmel (1858-1918) identified the 'Trickle Effect' (Simmel, 1957). A fashion is innovated by the elite and then 'trickles' down society until some mutated form of it is adopted by the underclass. In the meantime, the elite have innovated something else and the original innovation is no longer associated with them. In Early Modern England, the elite wore lots of gold. This has now trickled down to the 'chav' underclass and nobody 'middle class' would dream of wearing 'bling.' Sun tans were once associated with farm labourers. As these labourers moved into factories in smoggy industrial towns, suntans became associated with the elite, who could afford to holiday abroad. They 'trickled down' and are now, once again, associated with the underclass, especially in the form of 'fake tans' (see Hayward & Yar, 2006, for a discussion of 'Chavs')

There are many other examples. In the 1970s, tracksuits were a relatively elite form of dress, associated with the new fashion of jogging . . . not anymore. At that time, having a tattoo was a clearly sign of low socioeconomic status. But these were adopted by Hollywood actors and are now trickling back down. In the 1980s, it was obvious to many people that anyone with a tattoo would be a bit dodgy and that you should be careful around them. Such a policy now involves caution around a lot of people, especially those currently in their 20s.

Similarly, in most of Western Europe, the ability to speak English used to be a sign that somebody was highly educated and so likely relatively intelligent. But in the last 40 years, English usage has become so widespread that it is the *failure* to speak it (or even the failure to speak it fluently), if you are younger than about 70, which implies low intelligence and low education (see Dutton, 2010).

We need something more reliable than ever-changing sociological markers. We need something permanent that works everywhere in the world; in every culture, every age group, and in every race. This is physiognomy. We are, in fact, evolved to judge people by their appearances, meaning that doing so is very likely to be accurate because those who failed to do so didn't pass on their genes. Experimental evidence has shown that people regularly judge others' personalities by their facial features (Willis & Todorov, 2006), these judgements are concurred with by others (Highfield et al., 2009) and people do so cross-culturally, strongly implying that humans have evolved to do so.

Moreover, experiments indicate that the judgements are actually correct, as set out in a *New Scientist* article in 2009 (Highfield et al., 2009). In 1966, the article reported, psychologists at the University of Michigan conducted an experiment on 84 undergraduates who had never met. They had to sit in complete silence with each other for 15 minutes and rate each other on the Big 5 personality traits, simply by appearance. Each participant also sat a personality test. For three of these traits – Extraversion, Conscientiousness and Openness – the students' appearance-based judgements significantly positively correlated with the actual personality scores (Passini & Warren, 1966). Clearly, it would have been a better experiment if sociological factors, such as clothing and hair style were rigorously controlled for, but the result is certainly eye-opening. Accordingly, the experiment was repeated using mug shots and the results for Extraversion and Conscientiousness were replicated (Little & Perrett, 2007).

In this short book, we will aim to understand exactly which psychological traits can be judged from a person's face and body and how. In Chapter Two, we will look at the body itself. In Chapter Three, we will focus on the head and face. In Chapter Four, we will examine the hands. And in Chapter Five, we will look at criticisms of reviving physiognomy.

Chapter Two

Beach Body

'The millere was a stout carl for the nones;
Ful byg he was of brawn, and eek of bones.
That proved wel, for over al ther he cam,
At wrastlynge he wolde have alwey the ram.'
The Miller in the Prologue of *Canterbury Tales*.

1. Body Type and Personality

The kind of body you have is a sound indicator of the kind of personality you have. In general, in physiology, three body types are distinguished. These co-called *somatotypes* are extreme cases where the different traits correlate in a particular direction. Distinguishing these body types is, therefore, useful to permit predictions to be made and it certainly allows predictions to be made about sporting ability (see Dutton & Lynn, 2015). The features have been found to be to a significant degree genetic. These *somatotypes* are:

1. *Endomorph* (Fat). A rounded body shape (stocky, relatively short) characterized by relatively short limbs, large trunk, and fat in the abdominal and lower body region. Short neck, narrow shoulders, large chest, wide hips, underdeveloped muscles, but gains muscle easily. This body type is common among field athletes, such as hammer throwers.

2. *Ectomorph* (Slim). Tall, thin, linear body, construction.   Long extremities. Short upper body. Narrow chest and shoulders. Very lightly muscled. This body type is frequent among long distance runners.

3. *Mesomorph* (Muscular). A square, large head; muscular chest, narrow waist, and large shoulders; a large heart; heavily muscled arms and legs; and minimal body fat. Short trunk and long limbs. This kind of body type is prominent among footballers and sprinters.

These differences are noted with three numbers (1-1-1) in the order endomorph, mesomorph, and ectomorph. The higher the number, the higher on the given spectrum the body is. In general, the numbers range between one and seven. Within these categories there are sub-divisions to reflect the way in which people combine aspects of the three essential types, such as having relatively high body fat in combination with relatively long legs.

American psychologist William Sheldon (1898-1977) (Sheldon, 1940) originally developed this body-type taxonomy. He attempted to correlate body-type with personality and intelligence. In many respects, his taxonomy was similar to that of German psychologist Ernst Kretschmer (1888-1964) (Kretschmer, 1931). Kretschmer distinguished between *leptosomatic* (slim), *athletic* (muscular), and *pyknic* (fat). He associated each of these types with certain personality traits, suggesting that the pyknic was prone to depression and gregariousness, the leptosomatic was prone to schizophrenia while the athletic was the least prone to mental illness but, when he did suffer from it then it would be schizophrenia.

Sheldon developed this by forming three essential personality types which roughly paralleled Extraversion, low Conscientiousness, and high Conscientiousness/Neuroticism. He correlated somatotype ratings and personality scores. He found that endomorphs were the most extraverted, ectomorphs were the most conscientious and neurotic, and mesomorphs were the least conscientious. Sheldon's research has, of course, been criticized. But we will see shortly that his body types would seem to partly reflect differences in testosterone level and that personality correlates with this roughly as Sheldon's model would predict.

2. Fat and Thin Psychology

Why is 'fat' a social class issue? In modern Western societies, obesity is very much associated with poverty. The answer is not only that poverty makes you fat – because the cheapest foods are now the least healthy – but also that the traits which make you fat also push you towards low socioeconomic status.

Low SES is predicted, in particular, by low intelligence and low Conscientiousness (see Jensen, 1998 and Nettle, 2007). In addition, there is some evidence that people who are higher in Agreeableness (Conard, 2006) or who have a certain optimal level of relatively high Neuroticism tend to perform better at university (McKenzie et al., 2000). Being fat is predicted by many of these same characteristics. Low intelligence predicts being fat (Kanazawa, 2014). This is because the less intelligent have lower time preference: they would rather take the smaller but immediate reward than the longer-term but larger reward (Jensen, 1998). This means that they are less able to forego the immediate pleasure of ice cream for the future positive of not being overweight and diabetic. In addition, they are likely to understand less about healthy eating and simply possess less knowledge of what constitutes healthy food or a reasonable portion. Low Conscientiousness also predicts obesity because the essence of low Conscientiousness is poor impulse control (see Nettle, 2007). People who are low in Conscientiousness simply cannot help themselves. They will always have the extra slice of bacon, the second helping; the cake which they 'know they shouldn't.' And the third factor is Extraversion. Extraverts simply enjoy everything positive more, and this includes tasty (and thus unhealthy) food (see Nettle, 2007).

Accordingly, if someone is obese it can be inferred that they have low intelligence, low Conscientiousness, and high Extraversion. If they are obviously intelligent – this can be reasonably inferred simply from vocabulary, for example – then their obesity is likely to be a function of personality. If they are not especially friendly or gregarious then poor impulse control is a pretty likely candidate. It follows that the person who is 'slim' or who has maintained a healthy weight is going to be relatively high in Conscientiousness, low in Extraversion and relatively high in intelligence.

As for those who are unhealthily thin, or whose weight violently fluctuates, there is a body of evidence indicating that such people are high in Neuroticism (Cervera, 2003). They are mentally unstable, leading to a delusional body image, extremely low self-worth, depression and anxiety. Women are higher in Neuroticism than men (see Soto et al., 2011) and there is sound evidence that they are evolved to be more concerned about their appearance than men are. Men tend to primarily sexually select for fertile and healthy women. They have nothing to lose from the sexual encounter, so their evolved strategy is to have sex with as many women as possible and especially women who are fertile and healthy, meaning they are likely to produce healthy off-spring. It follows that they are attracted to signs of youth and simply to women who are good-looking because, as we will see later, this is associated with genetic health.

Though these factors are of course relevant for women, they have more to lose from the sexual encounter (they can become pregnant) and, as such, it makes sense – or made sense in our evolutionary history – for them to be attracted to men who could and would invest in the child and themselves. As such, women have evolved to be more interested in the males' socioeconomic status or potential to attain it, and evidence of his pro-social, cooperative personality and his intelligence, as these may imply he will be faithful and be a good provider (see Buss, 1989). This is why modern men 'strut' by wearing expensive clothes and driving flash cars. It is true that fast LH women will also be attracted to men who are likely to be good in fights, and so men who are muscular and tall (Buss, 1989). But, in general, it is women who have evolved to be more concerned with their own physical appearance – as this is what men will select for - and it is thus women who are prone to eating disorders. The ultimate example of this evolutionary dynamic can be seen in someone like Donald Trump: the very high status man gets the very good-looking woman; a good-looking wife who is much younger than he is.

3. The Muscle Man and the Weakling

Returning to Sheldon's theory, it actually fits quite well with what we know about testosterone. If we're going to be simplistic about it, the stereotypical male body is more mesomorphic while the stereotypical female body is more endomorphic. Compared to men, women of the same age have wider hips, shorter limbs, and less muscle. These reflect their lower average levels of the male hormone testosterone. Of course, there are all kinds of variation within sexes – there are masculine women and feminine men – but, broadly speaking, this fundamental difference exists.

Testosterone is one of the factors behind men looking different from women (Chang, 2002). More testosterone, however, means a lot more than a more mesomorphic body. Men who are high in testosterone also tend to be of shorter stature than those who are low in it. High levels of testosterone at a relatively early age have been shown to reduce stature (Nieschlag & Behre, 2013, p.323). This is presumably because – following the Life History Model we looked at in the last chapter - energy has been put into factors relating to short term reproduction, such as developing muscles and a sexually attractive body. It has therefore been directed away from growth.

The r-strategist has grown up quickly and ended-up shorter than the *K*-strategist who would have started later puberty and stopped growing at a later age. Testosterone is associated with low impulse control, and low levels of altruism (Mazur & Booth, 1998). So, the typical 'muscle man' – on the short side and mesomorphic – will be inclined towards being aggressive and selfish. And this can be discerned simply from the nature of his body.

By extension, the low testosterone male – taller and with a relatively feminine body type – is much more likely to be cooperative, kind-hearted and friendly. He wouldn't be much help to you if you got into a fight. But, due to his greater impulse control and altruism, he'd be less likely to get into a fight in the first place. And he'd be better at negotiating your way out of the fight which you may have gotten into. In much the same way, a female with a more masculine body is likely to be higher in testosterone and thus more aggressive and less cooperative than a more typically feminine woman. They would also be more competitive for status, another of the side effects of testosterone.

We would also expect the more masculine-looking person to have higher levels of autism traits. High functioning autism (or Asperger's) is characterised by a very strong ability to systematize (create and work out systems) but a very weak ability to empathise. Autistics are socially unskilled, obsessed with detail, and have little interest in other people. These characteristics are associated with high testosterone. Autistics are subject to elevated fetal steroidogenic activity, including elevated levels of testosterone, as evidenced by tests of their amniotic fluid (Baron-Cohen et al., 2015). Dawson and colleagues (2007) have shown that autism is associated with a distinct intelligence profile. Autistics score strongly on the Ravens test (which strongly tests systematizing) relative to scores on broader IQ tests, which include vocabulary tests, for example. They score on average 30 percentile points higher, and in some cases 70 percentile points higher, on the Ravens than they score on the Wechsler, which is a broader test.

So, we would expect those who appear masculine to not only be more aggressive and less altruistic but also to be more obsessive and more socially clumsy. The stereotypical high testosterone male is, of course, profoundly interested in subjects such as cars and sport, often to the point of obsession. I have a Facebook friend from school (a perfectly friendly chap, I should add) who really is the typical high testosterone male in terms of his looks: broad face, chiseled jaw (we will discuss the face in the next chapter), and muscular. In 9 years of being his Facebook friend, I don't think he's posted anything that doesn't relate to his beloved Tottenham Hotspur football team ('COYS!'), except very occasional family updates or anecdotes about celebrities he's had in the back of his cab.

4. Testosterone and Intelligence

Testosterone markers don't merely allow you an insight into personality. They also allow you to infer intelligence. They don't necessarily say much about 'general intelligence' but they do tell you something about intelligence abilities. As we have seen, in general if somebody is high on one kind of intelligence then he is high on all of them. However, there is considerable individual variation. Einstein had such fantastical Mathematical intelligence that he came up with an original proof of Pythagoras' theorem when he was 12. However, his linguistic intelligence was so awful that he failed the exam to get into the Zurich Institute of Technology (see Dutton & Charlton, 2015). In much the same way, males have better spatial and mathematical intelligence than females and part of the reason is testosterone exposure. Adult women who were exposed to particularly high levels of androgens in utero score significantly higher on spatial ability tests than do controls (Resnick et al., 1986) while there is evidence that testosterone level in healthy males is positively associated with spatial ability (Janowsky et al., 1994). Adrenal Hyperplasia is a condition where the adrenal gland is larger than normal and the body is missing an enzyme which causes this gland to release cortisol. The result is an increase in testosterone, which can lead to extremely masculine boys and extremely masculine girls. These girls tend to have high spatial intelligence (Resnick et al., 1986).

As such, we can reasonably expect that a man who evidences high testosterone will be better at spatial and mathematical than linguistic tasks. Likewise, a woman who appears masculine will be better at these tasks, at least compared to other women. I was at a conference at University College London in 2015. The university was trying to promote the idea that women have made an important contribution to science. The wall of the student refectory was decorated with photographs of living, relatively eminent female scientists who (if I recall correctly) were all working at that university. It was remarkable (to myself and my colleagues from the conference) how masculine the faces of these women scientists were. It was remarkable and entirely unsurprising.

5. Skin and Hair

Within races, skin and hair pigment is partly a reflection of testosterone. High testosterone levels are associated with high levels of melanin and thus darker skin and hair (Thornhill & Gangestad, 2008). Rushton and Templer (2012) found that among human races and animal sub-species darker pigmentation is associated with higher levels of aggression and higher levels of sexual activity. Moreover, they found that even within human races (such as when comparing siblings) darker siblings tended to be more aggressive and sexually active as well as less intelligent than lighter siblings. Females tend to find darker skinned men attractive; dark skinned men are higher in testosterone and thus implicitly more masculine and more fertile (Thornhill & Gangestad, 2008). Men tend to find lighter skinned women attractive in all cultures, partly because light skin implies fertility in women (perhaps because skin becomes lighter during ovulation). Light-skin is also attractive because it likely allows you to better perceive the marks of age; with age being an important dimension to fertility, especially in women. In addition, light-skin implies low testosterone in general. It is part of a syndrome of feminine characteristics. In so much as females are evolved to be feminine (and males evolved to be masculine) it implies, in essence, good genes, with very few mutations (Little et al., 2011).

Consistent with this, Lewis (2012) exposed 20 men who were white, black, and East Asian to 300 Facebook photos of university students aged between 18 and 30 from these three races. He found that, among students at Cardiff University, men of all races found East Asian women the most physically attractive, black women the least physically attractive and whites intermediate. Conversely, when the experiment was repeated with 300 photos of men, the 20 women of these races found black men the most physically attractive, East Asian men the least, and whites intermediate. Lewis hypothesized that a significant reason was testosterone, as expressed in average levels of femininity and masculinity and in coloration.

Of course, what this all means is that comparing people of the same age, race, and sex, we would expect the ones with darker pigmentation to be more aggressive and less altruistic. And this is because having darker skin and hair, in part, reflects higher levels of testosterone. It should also be noted that there is variation in what men and women find attractive based on the kind of relationship they are interested in, but we'll turn to this later.

6. Breasts and Other Body Ornaments

Darwin proposed two key kinds of selection. The first, which we might call individual selection, proposes that individual organisms that are the best adapted to their ecology are more likely to pass on their genes and so if an adaptive mutation arises then it will be selected for. Darwin also proposed 'sexual selection.' This is the idea that, within a species, certain individuals are found more attractive than others because they evidence greater genetic health. People want to copulate with these healthy specimens and they will shun those they find unattractive. In many social animals, males fight for the right to mate and the females, anyway, want to mate with the males who win these fights. This is because, by winning the fights, they are proving that they have the best genes and these will be passed on to the offspring.

Fighting, however, is not the only means of displaying genetic quality. Sexual ornaments are another. An obvious example of a 'sexual ornament' is a peacock's tail, highlighted by Geoffrey Miller (2000). This may have some use in terms of individual selection, in that the peacock can make himself look bigger to predators by displaying a particularly large tail. However, it is also a 'fitness indicator:' an indicator of good genes. A peacock with poor genetic fitness – and thus a high number of mutant genes – would have to invest more of its resources in simply staying alive than a peacock with fewer mutant genes. As such, it would not be able to grow or maintain as impressive a tail. The tail of a less fit peacock would be smaller, duller, less ornate and more asymmetrical. This is because we are evolved to be symmetrical, so symmetry shows that we have a lack of mutant genes which cause asymmetry and that we are fit enough to have grown a healthy phenotype in the face of disease or food shortage (Miller, 2000), hence 'symmetrical faces' are seen as attractive in all cultures: they evidence genetic health. The tail is also

31

a deliberate handicap, as it slows the peacock down substantially. As such, the peacock is advertising the fact that his genes are so fantastic that he can handicap himself, with this huge tail, and still have the resources left over to make it colourful and ornate. It's rather like a human male openly giving money to charity and, in so doing, stressing just how successful he is. He has money to burn.

With these considerations in the mind, the tail would tell the peahen a great deal about the fitness of the peacock and we would expect the peahen to (1) Select for peacocks that had a tail and (2) Select for peacocks with the largest and brightest tails. Miller argues that sexual dimorphism in humans – men and women looking different - can therefore partly be explained by sexual selection. This has obvious consequences in terms of physiognomy. The brain is incredibly sensitive to mutation. This is because it is an extremely complex muscle and 84% of our genes relate to the brain (Woodley of Menie et al., 2017). This means that if you can successfully grow an ornament, the fewer mutant genes you are likely to have in the brain.

Males are evolved to find female secondary sexual characteristics attractive. An ideal waist-to-hip ratio (WHR) is found to be attractive, for example. A very high WHR correlates with health problems and infertility while one that is too low will mean that the woman is starving, which will also lead to infertility (Davies, 2012, p.107). As such, an optimum WHR of around 0.7, in European cultures, is found the most attractive: that is a moderately curvy woman. Symmetrical and approximately average to slightly above average sized breasts are the most attractive (e.g. Havlicek et al., 2016). This is because they are an honesty signal of genetic health. Poor genetic health will manifest itself in asymmetrical, oversized or undersized breasts and buttocks and, in addition, average-sized but firm breasts seem to betoken optimal fertility (Havlicek et al., 2016). And if the female has this high mutational load then it is more likely that she has mutant genes which relate to brain functioning, implying – even if only very weakly – lower intelligence and higher mental instability. However, it must be stressed that breasts and even more so buttocks pale in into insignificance when compared to the face as the means by which female attractiveness is judged (Furnham & Swami, 2007). This is presumably because so much information on health, fertility and even character can be inferred from the face, so we are evolved to be particularly interested in it.

The male 'ornaments' are increased height (see below) and increased muscularity and so a total lack of muscle or extreme shortness would likely reflect mutation and thus general high mutational load. Other male ornaments include testosterone-influenced features, such as a manly chin and jaw and a larger penis (Weinbauer et al., 2013, p.54).

I have found one academic study which summarises research looking at the relationship between ornament size and personality (Steiner, 1980). It notes two key studies, both unpublished conference presentations by the American psychologist Nancy Hirshberg (1937-1979), who unfortunately seems to have been taken very young, and her colleagues. In these studies, the 144 subjects were female students at the University of Illinois. Large breast size was found to be significantly positively correlated with being 'undersocialized' (that is, antisocial), undependable, impulsive, 'psychologically minded' (that is introspective), flexible and adventurous. So, to some extent, the larger a woman's breasts are the lower in Conscientiousness she is, the higher in Extraversion she is and the less Agreeable she is. Women with large buttocks were found to be introverted, self-abasing, and high in guilt. In other words, they were relatively low in Extraversion and relatively high in aspects of Neuroticism. Another study highlighted by Steiner (Wiggins et al., 1968) involved 95 male subjects. It found that men who like small breasts tend toward being religious and depressive, and men who like larger buttocks are ordered, dependent, and 'self-blaming.'

Steiner (1980) observes the fascinating implication of this. Men who like big breasts are psychologically similar to the females who possess them, and the same is the case with men who like large buttocks. This would make sense in terms of Life History Theory, which we have already discussed. According to Rushton (2000) the faster a person's LHS is, the more pronounced their secondary sexual characteristics will be. This is because in an r-strategy context, essentially based around physical appearance, you are competing for the best mates and you need to attain them quickly. The larger your breasts are, the more you will stand out as potentially healthy and fertile, rather like with a peacock's tail. The male who was more attracted to larger breasts would thus be more attracted to the better quality females and would so pass on more of his genes. The female with larger breasts would be better advertising her fertility and genetic health, something that is relatively more important in a fast LH context, in which her psychological characteristics are of less importance.

Men who were more *K*-strategy would be less interested in secondary sexual characteristics – which would simply be a sign of health and (indirectly) fertility - and more interested in psychological characteristics which would produce a good mother and a loyal wife, who wouldn't have affairs and cuckold you. This would mean less of an arms race for large secondary sexual characteristics, so the population would have smaller breasts. In such a context, there would of course be individual variation. However, large breasts would betoken a faster LH, in which a person was genetically programmed to 'live for the now.' Small breasts would betoken the fact that the woman was less programmed to sexually advertise, meaning a slower LH. So, it would make sense for a slower LH man to be more attracted to smaller breasts in order to attain a slower LH female. In addition, we can see why a slower LH female would have smaller breasts. They are part of a constellation of slow LH traits. The slow LH female is programmed to invest less energy in sexual ornaments and more energy in her brain, and specifically in high GFP.

Returning to our earlier discussion of femininity, it is clear that what is attractive varies according to your LHS. A highly feminine face is attractive, in particular, in terms of a short term relationship where all a man wants to do is pass on his genes; meaning a healthy and fertile partner is all that is needed. However, if he's interested in a long-term relationship which requires investment on his part, then the personality of the female becomes much more important. He needs, after all, to ensure that the resulting child really will be his and that the mother will look after it, otherwise his investment is wasted. He may trade femininity for personality. And to the extent that being extremely feminine in terms of secondary sexual characteristics is associated with an r-strategy, he may actually start to find these traits less attractive. In addition, he may trade evidence of physical 'good genes' (such as a highly feminine face) for personality, at least within certain bounds.

This is consistent with evidence that high testosterone men are more drawn to women with highly feminine faces. Indeed, an experiment has shown that when men are exposed to a testosterone gel, they rate feminine faces as more attractive than they do when they are not exposed to this gel. In addition, the men preferred feminine faced women for short term relationships but this effect was more pronounced when they had been exposed to the testosterone gel. This is a very interesting set of findings. It implies that testosterone makes men more prone to a short term sexual strategy; valuing femininity highly. But it also makes them more concerned about being cuckolded in a long-term relationship; perhaps because it makes them less trusting. High T men, when it comes to a long term relationship, are more likely to trade femininity for other characteristics (Bird et al., 2016). It is unclear why this is so. One possible explanation may be that man are evolved to be deeply concerned about being cuckolded and the more masculine (high T) they are then the more concerned they are about this, rendering them more prepared to act to pre-empt it. So, in general, high T men are not interested in long-term, high investment relationships. But if they are told they must have one, then they want a strong insurance policy against cuckoldry. Low T men are more interested in long term relationships. But Rushton (2000) argues that *K* strategy involves being more 'group selected,' concerned not just about your family but the broader genetic group of which you are a part, which would effectively be a kind of genetic extended family (see Salter, 2007). Thus, a low T man will select for a reliable woman but he might also be far happier to, for example, adopt a child that is totally unrelated to him. Consistent with this, it has been found that people of low social status – which is associated, as we have seen, with a fast LH – are much less likely to adopt than are those of high social status (see Nickman et al., 2005).

Body ornaments are yet another situation where comparisons can only be made within races. Northeast Asian women, for example, tend to have relatively flat breasts and buttocks. This is likely partly an adaptation to the cold of Northeast Asia. The environment is so harsh that Northeast Asians had to focus strongly on survival, with insufficient resources left over for large ornaments and, moreover, any protrusion would potentially risk frostbite. Allen's Rule predicts that species from colder climates have shorter limbs, which retain heat, and large breasts would function as a limb. Further, any fat would be better off piling onto the stomach where it could act as a natural blanket rather than onto the buttocks. And, in addition, North East Asians are the most K strategy race, so we would expect them to have small secondary sexual characteristics for that reason alone.

7. Height

There are race differences in average height, in part due to a more stocky body type being more likely to survive in a very cold environment. But within races, there is a clear association between intelligence and height. On average, the cleverer you are, the taller you are likely to be, with a correlation of about 0.1 (Silventoinen et al., 2006). Historically, a big part of this was simply a function of wealth. More intelligent people were richer and had a better diet. Consequently, they reached their phenotypic maximum height while the less intelligent, who were less well-off, didn't. It is partly for this reason that kings like England's King Edward IV (1442-1483), who was 6 foot 3 and a half (1.61m), towered over the average man of the time, by almost a foot (Ross, 1974, p.10). Unsurprisingly, with the Industrial Revolution and eventual improvements in diet, average height started to increase as almost everyone reached their phenotypic maximum. In the UK, the average height increased up until the 1970s when it reached 5 foot 10 for men, slightly more than the 5 foot 8 (1.78m) average when we lived as hunter gatherers with a varied and healthy diet including lots of fruit and nuts (Winston, 2010, p.91). Since the 1970s height has plateaued, implying that we have reached our phenotypic maximum (Cole, 2003). We know that the height increase is a matter of environment because the growth has been on the less heritable aspects of height; specifically leg length. Leg length is strongly subject to environmental influences (Cole, 2003, Hatton, 2013).

Height is genetically correlated with intelligence (Silventoinen et al., 2006). Even when you control for environmental factors, the association still holds firm. The probable reason is that they have been 'sexually selected' (see above) for as a kind of bundle. Females have sexually selected for intelligent men (because intelligence predicts social status and they have specifically selected for this) but they have also selected for taller men, realising that taller men will be better able to protect them. This predilection for tall yet intelligent men has led to the two characteristics being associated with each other. As such, taller people are, on average, more intelligent than shorter people. Men may have selected, to a lesser extent, for taller over shorter women because shortness would imply poor genetic health; the inability to grow a tall body. Poor genetic health would also be associated with low intelligence.

8. Tattoos

It is worth mentioning the issue of body art, as it is of cross-cultural significance. In general, body art – such as tattoos – can tell one a great deal about the person who has permanently decorated their body. Tate and Shelton (2012) have found that when comparing those with tattoos to those without, those with tattoos tend to be weakly but significantly lower in Agreeableness and Conscientiousness. Indeed, Heywood et al. (2012), using a sample of over 8000 people, found that those with tattoos are more likely to take serious risks. This would be consistent with a fast Life History Strategy and with what tattoos appear to do. They draw attention to the body, they stress individuality or membership of a subculture, they display the ability to endure pain, and they draw attention to oneself. These characteristics are all associated with a fast Life History strategy.

The positioning and subject matter of tattoos only makes this clearer. Male tattoos are often on the arms, shoulder blades, and legs, so-stressing muscularity. Female tattoos are often on the small of the back (the so-called 'slag tag' or 'tramp stamp'), above the breasts, or on exposed flesh on the back of the neck. This is drawing attention to sexual parts of the body and titillating males with what's 'on offer.' In general, tattoos can be seen as a form of mutilation; a handicap – like the peacock's tail – which stresses genetic quality: 'I'm still attractive despite having mutilated myself, so think how good my genes must be.' They are also a form of deliberate asymmetry (a bit like skin disease), thus drawing attention to the individual's body. By having a tattoo, you are enduring pain and even risking blood poisoning, which is, again, consistent with tattoos as a means of advertising genetic quality, a point made in Lynn and Madeiros (2017, p.267)

The subject matter of tattoos would also seem to imply an r-strategy. In the case of men, it tends to be images of death, such as skulls, and subculture images such as nationalistic symbols. These seem to be ways conveying the idea that they are part of a gang and that they are brave: they're not scared of death. In the case of women, it is pagan fertility symbols of various kinds, the exotic (Chinese script and so on) as if to indicate child-like curiosity, or images that indicate a quirky, childlike attitude and so stress youth and thus fertility. For example, I once had a female student who had a tattoo of Little My, the naughty girl from *The Moomins,* on her left calf.

This is consistent with experimental findings that men assume that tattooed women are more promiscuous than non-tattooed women (Gueguen, 2013). Indeed, there is evidence from Poland that those with tattoos are slightly more sexually active than those without (Nowosielski et al., 2012). It should be added, however, that Swami et al. (2012) found that the tattooed had greater Extraversion, but none of the other differences on the Big 5 were significant. Both this study and Tate and Shelton found that those with tattoos had a greater 'need for uniqueness.' This is consistent with a fast LH as slow LH strategists strongly subsume themselves into the group.

Chapter Three

Talking Heads

'A somonour was ther with us in that place,
That hadde a fyr-reed cherubynnes face,
For saucefleem he was, with eyen narwe.
As hoot he was and lecherous as a sparwe.'
The Summoner in the Prologue of *Canterbury Tales*

1. Wide Boys

The shape of the face is yet another secondary sexual characteristic. High testosterone men will develop a muscular neck, a square jaw, and a furrowed brow. So these characteristics will be at least weakly associated with the personality characteristics of aggression and selfishness. The other facial marker of testosterone again requires that you control for race. Northeast Asians tend to have relatively wide faces. This reduces the surface area of their faces and so retains more heat in the cold environment to which they are evolved. But putting that aside, wide faces are associated with high testosterone. A study of ice hockey players found that those with the wider faces played in a more aggressive and selfish way and were more likely to break the rules (Carre & McCormick, 2008).

Low testosterone males will thus have narrow and more feminine faces. These kinds of faces tell women that such men are more likely to commit and more likely to want long-term rather than short term relationships (see Little et al., 2011). It is for this reason that studies have found that the extreme masculine face is often less attractive than a male face which indicates the desired optimum combination of masculinity (dominance) and femininity (cooperativeness, caring nature) (Little et al., 2011). There is, of course, individual variation – depending on the kind of man desired – with regard to what kind of face is the most attractive.

It is worth noting that a study by Kleisner et al. (2014) took facial photographs of 80 biology students and then measured their IQ. A sample of 160 people were then asked to rate the IQ of these faces. They found that their sample could accurately judge the intelligence of men from their faces, to a greater extent than would be possible by chance. However, they could not do so with women.

Kleisner et al. explain that 'a narrower face with a thinner chin and a larger prolonged nose characterizes the predicted stereotype of high-intelligence, while a rather oval and broader face with a massive chin and a smallish nose characterizes the prediction of low-intelligence.' However, they found that it wasn't factors such as face shape that were being used to judge intelligence, as these cues do not objectively correlate with intelligence. One possibility is that it could be a series of cues acting together or even the eyes (which we will discuss below) and perhaps the experiment should be repeated with people's eyes closed.

It is certainly interesting that the sample was able to judge intelligence from male but not female faces. The authors suggest a number of possible explanations including a 'halo effect' surrounding pretty females, meaning they are judged by physical attractiveness and this overwhelms intelligence cues. However, as we will see below, research by Lee and his colleagues (2017) would appear to rule this out. Another explanation is that it is more important to be able to judge intelligence from a male face, because females want to copulate with intelligent men when they are ovulating (in order to get good genes) but less intelligent though more honest or wealthier men when they are not ovulating in order to get a 'provider.' Men, by contrast, do not follow such a 'mixed' strategy.

Lee and his colleagues (2017) photographed 1,660 twins and their siblings, aged between 16 and 18. These were photographs of the face only, with a neutral expression. They had intelligence data for their sample. The photographs were then rated for intelligence by two groups of undergraduate research assistants. Lee and his team found that rated IQ did indeed weakly positively correlate with actual IQ, at 0.15. This persisted even when controlling for physical attractiveness, meaning that it cannot be put down to a 'halo effect.' So, people can accurately discern intelligence from a person's face and they can do so not only with adults – as in earlier samples – but also with adolescents. It is unclear how they are doing this, but Lee and his colleagues found that perceived intelligence is associated with a taller face height, a larger distance between the pupils, and having a larger nose. In addition, they found that those who had taller faces and a larger distance between their pupils were actually objectively more intelligent.

Lee and his colleagues have a number of intriguing suggestions regarding why these relationships may exist. They argue that mental impairment is associated with facial abnormality. It may be that we learn this and unconsciously judge people accordingly. Thus, having a small nose is associated with Downs Syndrome and Foetal Alcohol Syndrome and this would have contributed to our assuming that those with smaller noses were less intelligent. The correlations with objective intelligence could relate to this. Downs Syndrome and Foetal Alcohol Syndrome are major disruptions of developmental pathways and they lead to very low intelligence and a very small nose. Thus, even minor disruptions would lead to slightly reduced intelligence and a slightly smaller nose. The same could be said for distance between pupils and face height, which reached significance in terms of a relationship with objective intelligence.

Finally, Lee and his colleagues tested the extent to which the relationships they'd noted had a genetic component. Interestingly, they found that the genetic element was significant for men whereas the environmental component was significant for women. This is particularly fascinating in light of Kleisner's research finding that male intelligence could be objectively judged from the face but female intelligence could not. Lee and his colleagues suggest that females sexually select for intelligence to a greater extent than do males. It would, therefore, follow that there would be selection pressure on men (but not to the same extent on women) to develop facial cues for intelligence; to better advertise their intelligence.

2. 'Your Eyes are too close together!'

The personality characteristics associated with high testosterone – such as relatively low Conscientiousness – are also associated with criminality. We have already seen that Francis Galton created 'criminal' and non-criminal faces and found that they looked noticeably different. This was recently replicated, using modern techniques, by two Chinese researchers. Wu and Zhang (2016) used the faces of 1,856 real people and they controlled for the confounding factors of race, sex, age, and facial expression. Almost half of their sample was convicted criminals. Summing up their findings they write that their study, 'produce(d) evidence for the validity of automated face-induced inference on criminality, despite the historical controversy surrounding the topic' (Wu & Zhang,

2016, abstract). They also found that specific facial features were more common among the criminals than among the non-criminals. These were: lip curvature, the distance between the two eye inner corners, and the angle from the nose tip to the corner of the mouth (Wu & Zhang, 2016, p.6). They found that the angle, 'from nose tip to two mouth corners is on average 19.6% smaller for criminals than for non-criminals and has a larger variance.' In addition, 'the upper lip curvature . . . is on average 23.4% larger for criminals than for non-criminals.' However, the distance 'between two eye inner corners' is slightly narrower (5.6%) for criminals than it is for non-criminals.

So, putting it in simple terms, firstly, there is greater facial diversity among the criminal population than among the non-criminal population. This actually makes a great deal of sense, because we would expect the criminal population to be more genetically diverse. Understanding this requires something of an aside. Woodley of Menie et al. (2017) have proposed the so-called 'Social Epistasis Model.' They argue that up until the Industrial Revolution we were subject to intense natural selection. With a child mortality rate of about 40%, every generation mutant genes (which are almost always damaging) were continuously removed from the population. There would have been intense selection pressure on a number of psychological traits as well. There was selection on intelligence because this correlates with wealth and there is evidence that, in England in the seventeenth as well as in many other parts of Europe, the richer 50% had almost double the number of surviving offspring than did the poorer 50% (see Dutton & Charlton, 2015, for summary). Due to the relationship between GFP and socioeconomic status, this would have been selected for as well, as further evidenced by its relatively high heritability.

It has been argued that, eventually, we reached a point where average intelligence was so high that we produced geniuses – people of outlier high IQ – of such brilliance that the breakthroughs of the Industrial Revolution were made (see Dutton & Charlton, 2015). These breakthroughs, especially in medicine, led to the collapse of child mortality. Woodley of Menie et al. (2017) argue that this would have led to accumulation of mutations every generation and that these would have strongly impacted the mind, as the brain is 84% of the genome. They also note that physical and mental health correlate; when eighteenth century children with poor immune systems died it was also weeding out those who had mutant genes relating to the mind – it was removing mutation, in general.

It would follow that by 2018 almost 90% of the population of England wouldn't have existed in 1700; when the population was at its maximum for the agricultural ecology of about 6 million. And this 90% would be the mutants who would be lower in intelligence, lower in GFP, and higher in criminality. So, it makes sense that the criminals are more genetically diverse. Genetic diversity is a reflection of the collapse of Natural Selection.

As for their other findings, what they seem to imply is that criminals simply have less symmetrical faces than non-criminals. This makes sense, because we are evolved to be symmetrical. Facial symmetry correlates with health. So, we would expect those who wouldn't have survived under natural selection – including many modern day criminals – to have relatively asymmetrical faces. It is unclear why 'criminals' should have a more downturned upper lip. The closeness of their eyes can be understood in light of the findings of Lee and others (2017) which we explored earlier, combined with evidence that criminality is associated with low intelligence. But much as Wu and Zhang's study has been criticised (RT, 10th May 2017), it does seem to be broadly consistent with other research presented here.

3. Baldness

Baldness is yet another reflection of high testosterone, though only within races. Batrinos (2014) observes, based on a literature review, that baldness in males, known as androgenic alopecia, is positively associated with levels of testosterone. In this regard, eunuchs show no sign of hair loss even in old age. However, eunuchs who receive testosterone replacement therapy do eventually show signs of hair loss. In Pattern Baldness (PB), the hair loss is a result of an increase in the ratio of telogen to anagen hairs and the miniaturization of the hair follicle. The anagen phase becomes progressively shorter and the telogen phase becomes longer. Since the length of the hair is a result of the duration of the anagen phase, each hair becomes progressively shorter than its precursor. Eventually, the hair becomes so short that it does not reach the skin surface. In addition, because telogen hairs are not as well attached to the follicle as are anagen hairs, the increase in telogen hair count results in an increase of hair shedding in individuals with PB. With every completion of the hair cycle the hair follicle becomes progressively smaller, and thus the hair they produce becomes smaller as well. The scalp is left with only vellus hairs, which are very fine and lack pigmentation. High testosterone men are more likely to lose their hair and it is widely known among doctors – I base this on my own discussions with doctors - that males who come to them in their 60s complaining of impotence tend to have full heads of hair or only very limited hair loss. Again, this marker only works within races. If you compare races, then baldness is most common among white men, then Asians, and finally black men (Kolipakam & Kalish, 2007).

4. Don't be such a Big Head!

Intelligence is associated with a large brain, in comparison to body size, and it is also weakly associated simply with cranial capacity (see Vernon, 2000). In other words, intelligent people have big heads in comparison to the size of their body. This association is obvious at the extremes. People who suffer from a variety of conditions which reduce their intelligence, such as Foetal Alcohol Syndrome or the Zika virus, have noticeably very small heads. Francis Galton was the first to quantify the relationship between brain size and intelligence in living people. According to Rushton and Davison Ankney (2009), 'He multiplied head length by breadth by height and plotted the results against class of degree in more than 1,000 male undergraduates at Cambridge University. He reported that men who obtained high honours degrees had a brain size 2%–5% greater than those who did not.' They had large heads because they had large brains. Large brains, i.e. a bigger thinking muscle, means higher intelligence.

5. Not Much Behind the Eyes

It is commonly said that, 'The eyes are the window to the soul' and sometimes it said of a less than sparkling intellect that, 'There's not much behind the eyes.' We seem to somehow intuit intelligence from the eyes. Those who aren't very bright seem to have dull, blank expressions and these can be discerned from the eyes.

There is actually evidence that pupil size is weakly positively correlated with intelligence (Tsukahara et al., 2016). This actually makes a great deal of sense. The pupil is the interface through which the brain obtains information. The larger the interface, the more information it can obtain; as my colleague Michael Woodley of Menie has put it, 'the more bandwidth it has.' The more bandwidth it has, the quicker and more subtly it can solve whatever problem it is dealing with. And fast problem solving is the essence of intelligence. So, we would expect more intelligent people to have larger pupils. My colleague Bruce Charlton, a psychiatrist at Newcastle University, is not convinced, however. 'My inclination would be to look at things that reduced pupil size and diminished IQ/ IQ test performance; as being more likely causal than the opposite,' he tells me. In other words, perhaps there is something which both reduces pupil size and intelligence; one is not a product of the other.

It may also be that our response to the eye is something to do with blood flow and the ability to concentrate. Certainly, a vacant stare is one of the symptoms of concussion, that is, a trauma to the brain. Decreased cerebral blood flow is a significant dimension to concussion (Sprague-McRae et al., 2014, p.71). The possession of 'glassy eyes' is associated with a number of conditions. High blood alcohol level leads to glassy eyes (Thorburn, 2004, p.115), meaning that, when taken together with other symptoms, they may imply an alcohol problem and the personality factors which would predict that, especially low Conscientiousness (see Nettle, 2007). A vacant look is associated with Attention Deficit Hyperactivity Disorder (ADHD), other symptoms of which include inattentiveness, hyperactivity and impulsiveness (Engel, 2005, p.19). One of the symptoms of schizophrenia is a 'blank look' (Varcarolis, 2014, p.314), others being delusions, hallucinations, disordered thoughts, and pronounced irritability and anxiety. Bruce Charlton tells me sufferers from Parkinson's disease and those using certain anti-psychotic drugs have dull eyes. This is due to low levels of dopamine in the mesolimbic system. Lively eyes are an expression of high levels of dopamine.

A 'blank look' or 'glassy eyes' is also associated with 'dissociation,' which can be a response to feelings of intense stress (Darnall, 2013, p.83) and to psychological trauma (Gomez, 2012, p.133). Dissociation is a process whereby people are able to detach themselves from their surroundings. This can have a positive effect and, in particular, can reduce stress. At the non-pathological end of the dissociation spectrum sits day dreaming, and altered states of consciousness, such as religious experiences. In very pronounced cases, dissociation can manifest itself in multiple personality disorder. A traumatic memory might be suppressed (via dissociative amnesia) and if this unconscious memory is somehow 'triggered,' perhaps by feelings associated with it, then observers might see someone very suddenly adopting a very different persona (see Gomez, 2012). They might change from Dr Jekyll to Mr Hyde and the dissociation would be noticeable in the suddenly glassy eyes.

Some researchers, who have conducted fieldwork with fundamentalist groups or 'cults,' have observed something that I have termed 'eye glazing.' If they inadvertently manage to make the informant feel threatened, especially about their religious beliefs, then the informant may respond with a glassy stare. This is extremely unnerving and can be regarded as a boundary maintenance mechanism, because it will tend to make the perceived aggressor withdraw. I have personally experienced it three times, twice during fieldwork with fundamentalist Christian groups, but it seemed to stop happening as I became a more experienced fieldworker, meaning I became less prone to, as it were, 'cross the line.'

The first time it occurred was in October 1999, during Fresher's week at Durham University. I attended the Durham Inter-Collegiate Christian Union Chocolate Party, invited by the evangelical Christians who made up a third of my hall of residence (see Dutton, 2007). A third year student gave her 'testimony,' where she explained that she had met Jesus in the shower of my hall of residence, two years earlier. She ended by asserting that, 'I know my place in Heaven is secure.' Afterwards, I rather immaturely deposited the contents of my recently completed A-Level (school leaving certificate) in the Philosophy of Religion upon her and a 'glassy stare' was her response. Bruce Charlton has summarised glassy eyes in an interview for this book:

'One cause is delirium – brain dysfunction. The way I think of it is that attention is being diverted to inner-generated material – such as imaginary visions or waking dreams. So the person is no longer fully attending to the external environment - and that inattention shows in the eyes which they look 'vacant,' unfocused and roam around 'randomly'. Or the person may be distracted by internally-generated material such as hallucinations – and are staring in horror at something invisible, or grasping at 'dust' they see falling from the sky or ceiling. In less severe types of

46

delirium, people are characteristically 'perplexed' in appearance, and their eyes show milder but still perceptible signs of inattention and distraction.'

There are two other eye-related matters. The first is myopia or short-sightedness. This weakly positively correlates with intelligence (Verma & Verma, 2015), meaning that short sighted people – essentially most younger people who wear glasses – are likely to be more intelligent than those who don't wear glasses. The second is any kind of imperfection in the eye, such as a having a lazy eye. These are associated with, though not exclusive to, subjects with brain damage (Lewis & Bear, 2008). Brain damage is likely to be reflected in suboptimal intelligence and perhaps suboptimal personality.

The final important aspect of the eyes is width. Again, we must control for race here. Northeast Asians tend to have narrow eyes, seemingly as an adaptation against the sun dazzling off the snow in the prehistoric environment. Black people tend to have quite large eyes, certainly compared to Northeast Asians. But within races, narrow eyes are a reflection of high testosterone levels (Joiner & Kogel, Ch. 211). The ultimate low-testosterone human is the baby and babies, of course, are wide-eyed with wonder. Men tend to find neotonous (baby-like) features attractive in women, such as large eyes. This is because they imply low testosterone and youth and thus fertility (Buss, 1989).

6. Head Ornaments

It should be obvious by now but let's spell it out anyway. The ability to grow a nice, thick head of hair will reflect low mutational load. We would expect men to be attracted to long hair. This partly reflects attraction to health and fertility. Women at peak fertility are able to grow long, shiny, thick hair (see Goodwyn, 2012). Long haired women are rated more attractive, especially if they have long head hair on the periphery of the face, as this indicates peak fertility (Bereczkei & Mesko, 2007). It would thus follow – and it's widely observed – that older women tend to cover up the declining quality of their hair by cutting it short. Good hair could also be associated with general low mutational load, including in the brain. The same would be true of men.

However, the male ornament is more likely to be the beard. There are a number of theories with regard to evolution of beards, and they are likely sexually selected for as they are unlikely to be helpful in terms of Natural Selection. These have been summarised in Robb (5th February 2014). The first possibility is that they function as an honesty signal of genetic fitness, just as a peacock's tail does. They are clearly disadvantageous in fights and thus the hipsters with their Old Testament beards are showcasing their genetic quality (Zahavi & Zahavi, 1997). Related to this, beards are a clear advertisement of male health and status. They are a breeding ground for parasites, meaning that by having one you are demonstrating that you are resistant to these (Hamilton & Zuk, 1982). Thus, beards can be regarded as part of an r-strategy. Consistent with this, they have been found to make men look more aggressive, of higher status, and older (Dixson & Vasey, 2012), in a context in which females tend to be attracted to slightly older men, with age tending to be associated with status in men (Buss, 1989). Some studies have found that women find a modest level of beard growth more physically attractive than no beard (e.g. Reed & Blunk, 1990). This would seem to imply that a beard can be understood as a component of an r-strategy. It is advertising genetic quality and aggressiveness.

There are many aspects to hair length that might be explored. For example, in that men seem to be attracted to long hair, short hair on a young and attractive female could perform the same function as a peacock's tail: 'Look at me! I am attractive even with the attractiveness handicap of short hair!' However, a male sample rated women with long hair as 'healthy' and 'determined,' presumably because they could grow long hair, which the men found attractive. However, females with short hair were rated as 'honest,' 'caring', and 'feminine' (Bereczkei & Mesko, 2007). This would potentially imply that long hair is the r-strategy in women, because it is overtly showcasing genetic health. Short hair is being deliberately modest about showcasing health and, thus, is showcasing attractive personality characteristics. However, this is not the case with men, at least in Western societies. In this context, short hair is weakly associated with a more masculine personality (Aube et al., 1995). This would seem to make intuitive sense. A longer haired man is deliberately not advertising his masculinity. Indeed, he may be symbolically advertising the more feminine qualities of caring and trustworthiness; a *K* strategy, in other words.

7. Skin Quality

The main part of the body from which we judge genetic quality is the face. Women wear make-up in order to make themselves look younger and more symmetrical and cover up any skin conditions. But skin conditions are a direct or indirect reflection of mutational load. They are indirect in the sense that someone with a compromised immune system will have less healthy skin and their skin is more likely to be marked by childhood diseases such as chicken pox. Further, those who, due to low GFP or low IQ, consistently binge drink and eat unhealthily will find that this is reflected in prematurely aged and unhealthy-looking skin (see Parentini, 1995). And children who have poor impulse control and low Agreeableness are obviously more likely to disobey their parents and pick off their chicken pox scabs. This will, of course, sometimes result in a permanent scar and, if it's on their face where you can see it, it tells you something about their psychology even as adults. For example, a study using gene sharing in unrelated individuals confirmed that intelligence at age 11 genetically correlates with it in old age at 0.62 (Deary et al., 2012).

The kinds of chronic infectious diseases that are assumed to have been prevalent in hunter gatherer times (syphilis, yaws, TB) usually produce skin signs – and are transmissible to offspring. So signs of skin disease tend to be unattractive probably for evolutionary reasons, and lead to disgust, despite that the most common modern skin diseases (eczema and psoriasis) not being infectious.

8. Head Wounds

Even the slightest trauma to the head can cause brain damage and if it is significant enough to leave a scar or skull indentation then brain damage is essentially a certainty. Accordingly, if someone has a scar anywhere on the cranium we can make sensible inferences about how they are likely to react, particularly under stress or when tired. If the damage is to the frontal lobe – a scar anywhere on the forehead – it is likely to impact problem solving ability, concentration and personality (see Granacher, 2007 for a detailed discussion of brain injury). In particular, it can elevate levels of irritability and aggression. If it's anywhere else on the head, there's a fair likelihood it will be covered-up by hair. However, the fashion for prematurely bald men to shave off all their hair is quite helpful in this regard. I know such a man in Finland who speaks in a very unusual way. He speaks noticeably loud for a Finn, and with a very peculiar rhythm; almost staccato. One day I observed that he had a very deep scar on the side of his head, above his ear. Its position corresponded to the Parietal Lobe, the part of the brain which controls language.

9. Facial Symmetry

Across all cultures there is clear agreement on the kinds of faces which are found to be the most attractive. They are symmetrical faces. As we have discussed, this is because symmetry betokens good genetic health and low mutational load. They are also faces that are relatively average – in contrast to unusual – by population standards. This is seemingly because if ones features are close to the population average then one is genetically diverse, meaning one is more likely to have a low mutational load. Deviation from the 'norm' of the population would imply genetic distinctiveness and so, potentially, mutation (see Little et al., 2011).

There is an element to which 'beauty is in the eye of the beholder.' According to Genetic Similarity Theory, we tend to be attracted to opposite sex photographs when they are morphed to look like us. Couples are more similar than two random people from the same culture on numerous physical characteristics and particularly on the more genetic characteristics. We find people who are genetically similar to us attractive because by mating with somebody relatively – though not too – genetically similar to us, we pass on more of our genes (see Rushton 2005). Research from Iceland indicates that the 'sweet spot' for a long lasting, fertile and loving marriage is third cousin, or a non-relative with the same relatedness as a third cousin by genetic chance. Closer or further degrees of consanguity create less successful unions (Helgasson et al., 2008).

This would explain the subjective aspect to beauty, the reason why people will genuinely differ over whom they find attractive. For one man, a woman may be 'plain' while for another she is 'alright-looking.' But people tend not to differ at the extremes; with regard to who is found very attractive or very unattractive. This is because the objective factor in attractiveness is well-established. As discussed, it is symmetry and, in particular, facial symmetry. Not only does this betoken a low mutational load but it is associated with fertility (Little et al., 2011). And there is a weak but significant correlation between facial symmetry and intelligence (Kanazawa, 2011). On average, better-looking people are more intelligent. This is likely because low mutational load in the face is a proxy for having low mutational load in the brain. Also, similarly to intelligence and height the two traits may have been selected for as a 'bundle.'

Facial symmetry also permits insight into personality. Good-looking people tend to be higher in extraversion (Nettle, 2007). It has been suggested that this is because they have been treated well all their lives, so it's worth taking risks, this being a big part of extraversion (Nettle, 2007). It has been found that General Factor Personality – a social effectiveness measure combining the socially positive aspects of each of the Big 5 personality traits – is positively associated with physical attractiveness (Dunkel et al., 2016). In other words, good-looking people are more conscientious, more agreeable, more mentally stable, more extraverted and more creative than less attractive people. The simplest explanation would be that under conditions of harsh selection, intelligence, high GFP and genetic health (expressed in facial symmetry) provided a selection advantage (see Dunkel et al., 2017). And, as such, they have become genetically linked to each other.

It shouldn't be surprising that the face – as the most obvious honesty signal of genetic quality – conveys information about intelligence and character. Many genetic or epigenetic disorders, such as Downs Syndrome, Prada-Willi Syndrome and Foetal Alcohol Syndrome – partly express themselves via facial abnormalities of varying degrees of subtlety. Why wouldn't more subtle mental problems do the same?

10. Sexuality

The idea of the 'Gaydar' has become popular in recent decades. It refers to the ability to accurately discern whether or not somebody is homosexual, simply from what they look like. Often, sexuality is inferred from sociological cues, such as how people dress. However, there is evidence that it can be inferred with a degree of accuracy simply from what they look like. Kosinski and Wang (2017) extracted features from 35,326 facial images of different sexual orientations. They found that a computer programme they had designed could distinguish between gay and straight men with 81% accuracy and between lesbian and straight women with 74% accuracy. The results when using human judges were 61% accuracy with male faces and 54% accuracy with female faces. They argued that these accuracy rates were likely possibly because homosexuals have gender atypical facial morphology. In other words, homosexual men are more feminine than the norm while homosexual women are more masculine.

The gender difference in the accuracy rate is very interesting. It is consistent with evidence that sexual-orientation is much more genetic in men that it is in women. The available research on homosexuality indicates that it is around 0.39 genetic in adult men and 0.19 genetic in adult women (Långström et al., 2010). This, of course, implies that female sexual-orientation is more environmentally influenced than is male. And this in turn would explain why it would be less likely to be reflected in differences in facial morphology.

Once you identified a person's homosexuality, you can also make further reasonable inferences. Male homosexuality is associated with mental instability (Blanchard, 2008). It is also associated with a more feminine, low testosterone personality (Lippa, 2005) and more feminine intelligence profile (Rahman et al., 2017). Lesbians have a more male personality (Lippa, 2005) and intelligence profile (Rahman et al., 2017). They are, like their male counter-parts, relatively mentally unstable (Semlyen et al., 2016). A possible reason for this is that homosexuality is a sign of developmental instability and thus genetic mutation, evidenced in its association with numerous neurological disorders (Blanchard, 2008). The ability of an organism to buffer its development against environmental or genetic disturbances which it experiences during development such that it can produce a predetermined phenotype is known as 'developmental stability.' Mutant genes and poor environments will cause development to deviate away from the optimum, leading to unstable development, and potentially pathological outcomes (Nijhout & Davidowitz, 2003). Developmental stability is therefore likely to be very strongly related to underlying genetic quality, which in turn indicates evolutionary fitness. High mutational load is, thus, reflected in mental instability and abnormal sexuality being associated. Indeed, mental instability is even more pronounced among transsexuals (Blanchard, 2008), who can generally be easily identified by sight. In that exclusive homosexuality is lethal in terms of passing on your genes, it makes sense that it would be associated with mutation.

However, mutational load is only weakly associated with reduced intelligence (Woodley of Menie & Fernandes, 2016). To this end, it has actually been found that homosexuals have slightly higher average IQ than heterosexuals (Kanazawa, 2012). A possible explanation for this is that an aspect of problem solving, and thus intelligence, is the ability to be open to unlikely possibilities and thus the ability to rise above purely instinctive responses. The more open you are to superficially strange or unusual ways of thinking then the better you'll be at solving problems, which is why intelligence is positively correlated with the personality trait Openness. In addition, the better you are at suppressing your instinctive drives, the better you'll be at calmly reasoning through a problem. So, the smarter you are the stronger will be your attraction to evolutionary mismatch – to things which we wouldn't instinctively be attracted to. This would explain why Kanazawa (2012) finds that intelligence is correlated with numerous behaviours and ideas that would have been selected against under conditions of Natural Selection: atheism, low ethnocentrism and being nocturnal. It may therefore be that homosexuality is another example of this (Dutton & Van der Linden, 2017). Moreover, it can be argued that, in modern societies, intelligence is effectively maladaptive; hence its weak negative association with fertility (see Dutton & Charlton, 2015). Thus, it makes sense that intelligence would be associated with other maladaptive inclinations, such as homosexuality.

11. Ginger Hair

Chaucer's description of the Miller contained the usual stereotypes about people with ginger hair. The Miller is aggressive and temperamental and so it would have been no surprise to any of the pilgrims that he had ginger hair, and this what ginger-haired people were understood to be like. Pincott (16 April 2011) summarised the research on those with ginger hair in a very useful post in the magazine *Psychology Today*. People with ginger-hair are more sensitive to pain meaning they require 20% more anaesthetic than non-gingers (Liem et al., 2004). They are also more sensitive to cold (Liem et al., 2005). This is because the same gene which causes one to have red hair – MCIR.3 - is also involved in pain perception (Pincott, 16 April 2011). We would expect people who were in pain to be more temperamental and this kind of research explains why and provides empirical backing, indirectly, for stereotypes about ginger-haired people.

Chapter Four

Cross My Palm with Silver

'Jacob answered his mother Rebekka, 'But Esau my brother is a hairy man and I am a smooth man' (Genesis 27: 11).

Palmistry, like phrenology, is quackery. But hands are certainly very useful when it comes to understanding the kind of personality that somebody is likely to have.

1. 2D:4D Ratio

One widely acknowledged indicator of androgen (i.e., male hormone) exposure in utero is the so-called 2D:4D finger index ratio reflecting the ratio between the lengths of the index finger to the ring finger (Manning, 2003 or Manning & Fink, 2011). The 2D:4D ratio is often assumed to reflect the organizing effect of in utero exposure to androgens, mainly testosterone. A lower index implies higher exposure to testosterone. The 2D:4D index ratio is correlated with genetic variation in androgen receptors (Manning et al., 2003). Males with receptors that are less sensitive to testosterone have higher digit ratios. In other words, if the profile of someone's fingers is smoother, more like a shovel, then it implies high testosterone. If, by contrast, the little finger is significantly smaller than the middle finger, which is highly prevalent among women, then it implies lower testosterone exposure. Unsurprisingly, in light of our earlier discussion, autism is associated with a low 2D:4D ratio (Baron-Cohen, 2002). Very feminine hands, in both sexes, are associated with schizophrenia (Arato et al., 2004).

A high 2D:4D ratio is also associated with homosexuality, sexual fetishes, trans-sexuality, and paedophilia. It is unclear exactly why this is the case but Blanchard (2008) has suggested elevated exposure to female hormones in utero. The more older brothers a boy has, argues Blanchard, the more a mother produces these hormones meaning that having a large number of older brothers predicts homosexuality. By contrast, there is evidence that elevated exposure to testosterone in the early development of females is associated with elevated levels of, at least, not being exclusively heterosexual (see Hines, 2011).

2. Hairy Fingers and a Hairy Chest

High levels of androgenic hair are associated with androgen levels (Hamilton, 1958). One well-known proxy for level of androgenic hair is mid-Phalangeal hair (hair on the middle segment of the 4th digit or ring finger). A number of reviews and meta-analyses have brought together available data on the average level of Mid-Phalangeal hair in various countries (Hindley & Damon, 1973; Westlund et al., 2015). So, hairy fingers in men are a sound indicator of high testosterone. This would seem to extend to hairiness in general. This can be seen in Genesis with the brothers Jacob and Esau. Esau, who is 'a hairy man,' is the more aggressive and uncultured of the two. This is, once more, only a marker within races. There are racial differences in hairiness. Black people, for example, are less hairy than white people. It has been suggested that Neanderthal genes may be behind the relatively hairy nature of white people (Dutton et al., 2016).

3. Left-Handedness

What hand someone writes with – or, even better, waves with – will allow you to make cautious inferences about their psychology. Early research indicated that left-handers might be overrepresented among those with above average scores on specific measures of cognitive ability (Benbow, 1986; Halpern et al., 1998). However, a consistent pattern is emerging across studies with large samples and measures of general intelligence indicating that, on average, left-handed people are at a mild cognitive disadvantage relative to right-handers (Goodman, 2014; Johnston et al., 2013; Nicholls et al., 2010), and that this translates into real-world differences between the groups in terms of things like earnings (Goodman, 2014). So, those who have very high but narrow intelligence; where there are extraordinarily intelligent at just Maths, for example (Isaac Newton is an example) have elevated levels of left-handedness. However, in general, left-handed people are less intelligent than right-handed people.

One theory (see Markow, 1992), is that left-handedness results from reduced developmental stability. Hence elevated rates of left-handedness are associated with several indicators of developmental instability, including autism (Soper et al., 1986), schizophrenia (Dragovic & Hammond, 2005), immunological disorders

(Geschwind & Behan, 1982), psychosexual aberrations such as sexual fetishes (Rahman et al., 2007), paedophilia and homosexuality (Blanchard, 2008). Among homosexuals, left-handedness is far more prevalent among those who take the submissive role than it is among those who take the dominant role (Swift-Gallant et al., 2017). Left-handedness means that, in general, you are using the right hemisphere to process language, where animals and most people use the left side (Corballis, 2003). Over-use of the right hemisphere is associated with mental instability (Hecht, 2005). So, left-handedness means that something has gone wrong in development or genetically.

4. Taking Things Further ...

I earlier mentioned the concept of eye-glazing and how I first experienced it as an undergraduate, during a heated discussion with a member of Durham University's fundamentalist Christian Union. Unsurprisingly (considering the positive relationship between religiousness and GFP) I ended-up making many female friends who were Christians. In particular, I had many female Christian friends.

Research has found that, when it comes to opposite sex friends, the male tends to primarily find his female friends physically attractive. By contrast, the female is primarily attracted to the psychological aspects of the male friend: it is his character that she finds most attractive (Bleske-Rechek et al., 2016). This is entirely consistent with the broader finding that males having nothing to lose from the sexual counter and thus may as well be promiscuous and copulate with as many healthy (and thus good looking) women as possible. Thus, males are evolved to focus on physical attractiveness in finding a mate, though psychological characteristics are also relevant. Females are evolved to prize psychological characteristics over physical ones (Buss, 1989). Thus, the dynamics of opposite sex friendships are very similar to those of sexual relationships: the opposite sex friends, as it were, 'like' each other, but not quite enough. Bleske and Buss (2000) found that the female friend sees herself as getting physical protection and investment from the male (which the male sees as costs) while the male gets a potential sexual partner (which the female sees as a cost). Both sexes get somebody agreeable and dependable (Lewis et al., 2011). Interestingly, the male was more likely to still regard the relationship as merely a 'friendship' once it had turned sexual, implying that part of the motivation is sex without commitment – a 'friend with benefits' (Bleske & Buss, 2000).

Anyway, one thing that was noticeable about these Christian girls at university was that they were very good-looking. Indeed, 'Non-Christian' male friends of mine also commented on this. This got me thinking: Can you identify religious people using physiognomy or at least work out who is likely to definitely not be religious?

Religiosity is a syndrome of characteristics and identifying it is a very useful way of finding kind and trustworthy people, no matter what someone like Richard Dawkins might say. Religious people tend to have a relatively strong sense of identity, meaning that it is often possible to identify them from clear religious markers, such as the wearing of crosses in the case of Christians, especially when combined with relatively modest dress and low levels of make-up in the case of females (see Dutton, 2008 and Davies, 2002). Religiousness is associated with high General Factor of Personality (Dunkel et al., 2015) and, as we have seen, GFP is positively associated with physical attractiveness (Dunkel et al., 2016). This means that, in general, religious people, compared to atheists, are more Agreeable, more diligent, more outgoing, and more mentally stable. They are, by most measures, preferable to be with, at least in everyday situations. And there is a degree to which they can be identified simply from their physiognomy.

A systematic literature review by Dutton et al. (2017) has argued that until the Industrial Revolution we were evolved to accept a very specific form of religiosity: belief in a moral god and collective worship of this god. Religiousness, it shows, is about 0.4 genetic. It has been individually selected for because it reduces stress and makes people more moral, so they are less likely to be killed by the band. It has been sexually selected for because it's a marker for high GFP and an insurance policy against cuckoldry and desertion. And it has been group selected for because it predicts ethnocentric behaviour and, in computer models, more ethnocentric groups always eventually dominate. Thus, until the Industrial Revolution, religiousness was strongly selected for and it was a specific kind of religiousness: belief in moral gods coupled with collective worship of these.

The Industrial Revolution slowly weakened selection. It introduced better medicine, cheaper food, better sanitation, and generally superior conditions. Child mortality fell from 40% in 1800 to about 10% by the late nineteenth century and it's now at about 1%. Until the Industrial Revolution, those born with mutant genes – leading to mental and physical abnormality – died young, before they could pass on their genes. This has decreasingly happened for generations, argue Woodley of Menie et al. (2017). This has led to increasing 'mutational load' and consequently more and more people who, for genetic reasons, think in ways that would have been maladaptive in the past. They begin to influence society, undermining its traditional structures such that even those who don't carry the mutations begin to think in these ways. Dutton et al. (2017) have shown, in accordance with this model, that ways of thinking that are deviations from that which was the norm at the time of industrialization – such as atheism or belief in the paranormal but not in god – are associated with accepted markers of mutation. Atheists are more likely to be left-handed, autistic, homosexual or transsexual and have poor mental and physical health. Paranormal believers show elevated levels of schizophrenia and plain physical ugliness.

However, there are many other associations, most obviously skin condition. Rule et al. (2010) have shown that people in the USA can accurately distinguish Mormons from non-Mormons due to a so-called 'Mormon glow': the skin of Mormons looks healthier. It is unclear to what extent this is a reflection of the Mormon eschewal of alcohol, tobacco and coffee, rather than something genetic. But perhaps this 'Mormon glow' is indeed partly genetic in origin, something consistent with it already being evident on student (young) samples. Either way, it is likely to extend to the religious in general, helping them to be identified, especially in the case of females, who are less likely to wear make-up than atheist females. I once had a student from a fundamentalist group in Finland called the Laestadians. She wore no make-up, had perfect skin and spoke relatively poor English for her age (22) and education level. From this information I correctly guessed that she was Laestadian. They reject alcohol, makeup, and television (hence the deficient English).

In addition, there is evidence that this can be extended to what are broadly called left-wing people or, in the USA, 'liberals.' It has been found that Republican voters are more physically attractive than Democrat voters (Peterson & Palmer, 2017). Berggren et al. (2017) have found that in Europe, the USA and Australia, people rate 'right wing' politicians as more physically attractive than 'left wing' politicians. The authors provide an economic explanation: 'Politicians on the right look more beautiful in Europe, the United States and Australia. Our explanation is that beautiful people earn more, which makes them less inclined to support redistribution.' The problem with this argument is that there is far more to being a 'right-wing' politician than not supporting economic socialism. The current consensus in psychology is that two broad dimensions are necessary to describe sociopolitical attitudes (Duckitt et al. 2002). One of these is 'resistance to change' or 'traditionalism' and the other is 'anti-egalitarianism' or justification of inequality. Bergman et al.'s interpretation does not explain why good-looking politicians are more likely to be traditionalist. An alternative explanation to Berggren et al.'s, which is far less question-begging, is that egalitarianism, the questioning of religious tradition and the promotion of Multiculturalism (that is Leftist ideas) would have likely been met with horror by populations that lived under harsh conditions of Natural Selection. Populations which were so low in ethnocentrism as to espouse Multiculturalism and reject religion would simply have died out. It therefore follows that the espousal of leftist dogmas would partly reflect mutant genes, just as the espousal of atheism does. This elevated mutational load, associated with Leftists, would be reflected in their bodies as well as their brains. Accordingly, we would expect them to have higher fluctuating asymmetry in face – reflecting mutation – and this is indeed the case. In addition, there is a substantial degree to which 'religiousness' crosses over with being 'right-wing' in industrial societies. Indeed, the Right Wing Authoritarian Scale (RWA) and the Fundamentalism Scale have been shown to significantly correlate at 0.75 (Laythe et al., 2001). This further demonstrates that Leftism, of which atheism is effectively a dimension, is a reflection of high mutational. Under conditions of harsh selection, modern Leftists, like atheists, would die before they could breed or would never have been born.

Chapter Five

All in the Mind?

A number of scholars have taken issue with the revival of physiognomy. These criticisms take a number of forms.

1. Overgeneralization

Most prominently, Leslie Zebrowitz, reported in Highgfield et al. (2009), maintains that many of our instinctive, immediate judgements are not actually accurate. He argues that when we make such generalizations we are ascribing to the subject the qualities which we associate with certain archetypes. These are the qualities revealed by facial cues that are related to low fitness, babies, emotion, and identity. Zebrowitz and his team claim that these are 'overgeneralized' to: 'people whose facial appearance resembles the unfit (anomalous face overgeneralization), babies (baby face overgeneralization), a particular emotion (emotion face overgeneralization), or a particular identity (familiar face overgeneralization)' (Zebrowitz & Montepare, 2008, abstract). Thus, they argue, we associate facial malformation with disease and thus react to an unattractive person as though they are diseased. Similarly, we assume that babies are submissive so we react to a baby-faced person as though they are. The obvious rejoinder to this is that there is indeed evidence that facial symmetry is associated with a low General Factor of Personality and having a baby-like face is indeed empirically associated with being submissive. Moreover, if these reactions are instinctive, which seems to be the case, then they would have been evolved for under conditions of selection. Those who reacted adaptively, that is correctly, would simply have been more likely to have survived to pass on their genes. So, Zebrowitz's criticism can be satisfactorily dismissed.

2. Only the Kernel of a Model

Todorov and Oosterhof have also been critical of the line of research which we have explored. They argue that our judgements actually relate to how threatening faces appear. Todorov and Oosterhof (2008) asked people for their instinctive reactions to pictures of emotionally neutral faces. They went through all the responses, and found that there were two underlying factors behind the reactions: trustworthiness and dominance. They then worked out exactly which facial expressions or features were associated by people (positively or negatively) with trustworthiness and dominance. The researchers then used a computer programme to generate random faces which they morphed into caricatures of trustworthy, untrustworthy, dominant or submissive. They then asked subjects to ascribe emotions to the faces. The subjects consistently reported that the trustworthy faces were happy and the untrustworthy ones were angry. They regarded the dominant faces as masculine and submissive ones as feminine (Oosterhof & Todorov, 2008, summarised in Highfield et al., 2009).

Based on these findings, the authors argue that we may be overgeneralizing but there is clearly a 'kernel' of truth in people's reactions. It can be responded that there is far more than a kernel of truth and that the authors' experimental design may be to blame for the discrepancy. Intuiting personality from a face is bound to involve many interacting subtle cues. By presenting subjects with caricatures of particular cues, which the authors have concluded mean something very particular, they are not replicating that to which people would be evolved to react. Accordingly, their experiment should not lead us to the conclusion that we are prone to overgeneralize in any significant way.

3. Weak Correlations

It may also be argued that the correlations involved in physiognomy are often weak. For example, the correlation between intelligence and facial symmetry is about 0.1. It can be responded that the purpose of any system of categories is to allow successful predictions to be made, so better allowing us to negotiate our way through life. If the correlation is weak but statistically significant (meaning it is not simply a matter of chance), then it is a real relationship and it is evidence of the practical usefulness of physiognomy. Physiognomy will allow successful predictions to be made more often than would happen by chance. It is up to reader how cautious or reckless they wish to be based on the information which has been presented. Also, effect sizes in psychology tend to be quite weak in general; the norm being between about 0.1 and 0.3. So research on physiognomy is no weaker than that in many other areas of psychology.

Moreover, though many of the correlations may be weak on individual measures, if all of these measures cluster together – as they often do – then you have very reasonable grounds for making an informed judgement about psychology based on appearance and this is a superior judgement to one merely based on instinct or no judgement at all. Just because someone has a ruddy complexion it doesn't mean they are an alcoholic. However, if this is part of a syndrome including dry skin, burst capillaries, puffiness, yellowing of the eyes, blood shot eyes, and psoriasis on the hands . . . then it may well do. The same is true, for example, with measures of testosterone or physical indicators of low intelligence. Of course, once we actually get to know a person then we can understand their psychology first-hand and the need to judge them by their appearance evaporates. Thus, physiognomy is – in a practical sense – useful when dealing with people we don't know very well. It might be argued that even if a person does very much look like an alcoholic, people can deviate strongly from the norm of any group to which they are assumed to belong and so any judgement can potentially be extremely unfair. In dealing with a similar criticism Madison and Ullén (2012) have responded with three points. The first is simply 'a reality check.' In many situations the time in which you have to make a decision is 'severely limited' and you have to make it based on the available information: It's dark. There's someone walking towards you. You can see what kind of face and build he has. It implies certain things about him. What do you do? Secondly, they note that accepting a 'stereotype' will not necessarily involve unfair treatment. We can easily accept, they explain, that men are, on average, taller than women, without expecting every man we meet to be taller than every woman. Thirdly, they note that the consequences of judging in these ways cut both ways. Sometimes people will end up being treated more positively than would have occurred if we had simply got to know them. But the key point would seem to be practicality. Understanding the relationship between physical appearance and psychology helps us to make correct judgements, particularly in extreme situations when a quick decision must be made. These were often the situations in ancestral times. Psychopaths had to be avoided.

It might be argued that there will always be an intuitive dimension to such judgements because you can't go up to every man you meet and measure the width of their face. However, it can be countered that there is a difference between making an intelligent estimation of a measurement and merely intuiting it, as a kind of instinct. From a pragmatic perspective, we have to be able to make such quantitative estimations or we could never cross the road if there was a car in the distance.

4. What is the Direction of Causation?

A further criticism relates to the direction of causation. It has been suggested that the 'self-fulfilling prophecy' may explain why what we regard as masculine faces are associated with aggressiveness (see Highfield et al., 2009). In other words, society expects masculine-looking children to be aggressive, gives off cues that they should be, and so they become aggressive. This begs the question of why 'society' should believe that children with masculine faces should be aggressive were it not for the fact that they normally are. It ignores the strongly genetic nature of personality and the fact that masculine facial features are associated with elevated testosterone levels, increases in which make people more aggressive and so more typically 'masculine.' In addition, those who are more masculine tend to have genetic markers of this, such as lower 2D:4D ratio and even a different form of the androgen receptor gene, which affects levels of testosterone (Manning et al., 2003). It is most unlikely that being treated in a more masculine way will alter your genes to make you more masculine. What is far more likely is that those who are masculine are masculine partly for genetic reasons.

5. Is Physiognomy Morally Wrong?

Some readers may aver that it is simply wrong to judge people by their appearances. Following the Golden Rule, they might argue, 'You wouldn't want to be judged by your appearance so you shouldn't judge others by their appearance.' It can be countered that this kind of position is inconsistent. If we start from the pragmatic foundation that in order to survive we must be able to avoid the those who would do us serious harm, and if we further accept that – with some people – once you're talking to them in sufficient detail to discern their personality then it's too late, then it must follow that we have to be able to judge people by their appearance. And, of course, we do so all the time. The information presented here simply allows us to be more systematic, detailed, and logical in so-doing, leading to a more accurate and fair judgement; one based on the empirical data.

In addition, let us be consistent. It is very common in psychology to find a correlation between, for example, a certain behaviour and accidents (or health) of 0.15 or 0.2 and thus argue that action should be taken based on the results. These effect sizes are considered large enough to be meaningful and even for policy to be changed. The situation with the results we have explored here is very similar.

6. 'Careful Now . . .'

However, there are three areas that require caution. The first is using physiognomy on people of a different racial group from your own or on people from a racial group with which you have relatively limited contact. Coetzee et al. (2014) used a sample of Scottish (white) and black South African men and asked them to rate the attractiveness of various black female faces. They found strong cross-cultural agreement on the most attractive female face. However, the Scottish evaluators preferred thinner and less robust faces and tended to use facial shape, rather than skin tone, as their primary means of judging attractiveness. South African blacks preferred thinner/less robust faces as well, but their preference was less extreme. They were also more likely than the whites to use skin-tone in judging attractiveness. Coetzee et al. note that the lower exposure of Scots to African faces may render them less able to distinguish between these faces and thus less able to read cues for poor health or for infertility. To a lesser extent, this problem may arise even when we judge faces from our own race, though from an ethnicity to which are not accustomed.

This 'problem' is consistent with the common observation, by British men, that women from essentially any European country (with the possible exception of Ireland) are 'well fit.' I have heard Brits refer to Icelandic girls, Finnish girls, Italian girls, Latvian girls . . . girls from any country other than their own (or ethnic kin nations such as Australia) . . . as being extremely beautiful. This attitude is exemplified in the fly-on-the-wall documentary 'What Happens in

Sunny Beach . . .' which follows the antics of young British tour reps working at the Bulgarian resort. The reps, especially the male reps, are extremely promiscuous and, in particular, they aim to have sex with women from as many countries as possible, so that they can accrue the most 'flags.' One of the reps exclaims: 'I kind of look at myself as a young Adolf Hitler. I want to conquer Europe!' Another remarks: 'I had a Russian girl last year. That was absolutely amazing, to get my Russian flag in . . . I've had an Israeli girl as well, that was also a very, very nice flag to get . . .' This is because there aren't many Russians or Israelis at Sunny Beach. Albanians are a particular rarity such that if you find one, 'it doesn't matter whether she's 50 stone or 3 pounds you've gotta bang her to try and get the flag off the list' (*What Happens in Sunny Beach . . .* , Series 1, Episode 1). One possible explanation for this is that people from a different ethnicity will have different genes and this genetic diversity will mean that any resultant children are less likely to have genetic problems caused by recessive mutations being present in both parents. So, balancing this with the Genetic Similarity Theory we discussed, this may render us evolved to be attracted to foreigners, especially in the context of a fast Life History Strategy which sexual relationships in Sunny Beach are almost certain to be. Another explanation is that we are less able to read the signs of poor health (i.e. low attractiveness) in foreigners, because we are less used to them, and, thus, we are simply less discriminating.

7. Clever Tricks

The final reason for caution is people's ability to disguise their appearance. This is, of course, especially prevalent with females who use make up, and plastic surgery to alter their faces in order to make them more attractive. Fortunately, it is usually obvious when a woman is wearing a lot of makeup and it is certainly obvious when they have had plastic surgery. Or, at least, it is assuming that you are sober and the level light reasonable, which may not be the case in a night club. As such, this simply becomes a route into their psychology. Being dissatisfied with your body to the extent of presenting for cosmetic surgery has been found to be associated with a series of mental disorders. Indeed, 47% of those who present for cosmetic surgery have been found to have one and we can assume that many others are on the same scale but not high enough to be classified as mentally ill. One of the most common is Narcissistic Personality disorder – which is partly a reflection of low Agreeableness. Another is Histrionic Disorder. This is characterised by excessive attention-seeking and an excessive need for approval (Malick et al., 2008). Wearing make-up appears to boost women's self-confidence and reduce their social anxiety, so low self-confidence and high anxiety may be features of women who wear conspicuously large amounts of makeup, at least when controlling for factors such as age and attractiveness (Cash & Cash, 1982). Consistent with this, there is evidence, from a female sample, that having a positive image of one's body – likely to be reflected in relatively low levels of beauty augmentation – is associated with low Neuroticism (Swami et al., 2013).

8. Conclusion

We have referred to Chaucer's *Canterbury Tales* a number of times. In the General Prologue, Chaucer describes how a group of pilgrims – all of them on their way to the shrine of St Thomas Beckett in Canterbury – meet up at 'the Tabard,' an inn in Southwark (now in south London), on the pilgrimage route. They decide to travel together to Canterbury in a large group. Chaucer describes the physical appearance of each of the pilgrims, as well as providing the reader with any background information he has learned about them while staying at the Tabard. The standard reading of this is that Chaucer deliberately employs physiognomy in creating his characters, because that's what the Medieval reader expected. An alternative, and perhaps more likely, interpretation is that the characters were vaguely based on people Chaucer had met. And their physiognomy tended to be in line with their personalities because, in general, people's physiognomy is broadly in line with their personalities. *Canterbury Tales* is so successful, and can enrapture the reader, because people really are like that. It is often said that although Chaucer's characters are Medieval they are timeless. With those characters about whom we have detailed information this is true. And part of the reason for this is that their bodies and faces match with their characters.

References

Arato, M., Frecska, E., Beck, C., An, M. & Kiss, H. (2004). Digit length pattern in schizophrenia suggests disturbed prenatal hemispheric lateralization. *Progress in Neuro-Psychopharmacology and Biological Psychiatry,* 28: 191-194.

Aristotle. (1989). *Prior Analytics.* Trans. R. Smith. Indianapolis: Hackett Publishing.

Aube, J., Norcliffe, H. & Koestner, R. (1995). Physical characteristics and the multifactoral approach to the study of gender characteristics. *Social Behavior and Personality,* 23: 69-82.

Baron-Cohen, S., Auyeung· B., Nørgaard-Pedersen, B. et al. (2015). Elevated fetal steroidogenic activity in autism. *Molecular Psychiatry,* 20: 369-376.

Baron-Cohen, S. (2002). The extreme male brain theory of autism. *Trends in Cognitive Sciences* 6: 248-254.

Batrinos, M. (2014). The endocrinology of baldness. *Hormones,* 13: 197-212.

Baumbach, S. (2008). *Shakespeare and the Art of Physiognomy.* Penrith: Humanities E-books.

Benbow, C.P. (1986). Physiological correlates of extreme intellectual precocity. *Neuropsychologia, 24*, 719–725.

Bereczkei, T. & Mesko, N. (2007). Hair length, facial attractiveness, personality attribution: A multiple fitness model of hairdressing. *Review of Psychology,* 1: 35-42.

Berggren, N., Jordahl, H. & Poutvaara, P. (2017). The Right Look: Conservative Politicians Look Better and Voters Reward It. *Journal of Public Economics*, 146: 79-86.

Blanchard, R. (2008). Review and theory of handedness, birth order, and homosexuality in men. *Laterality,* 13: 51-70.

Bird, B., Welling, L., Ortiz, T. et al. (2016). Effects of exogenous testosterone and mating context on men's preferences for female facial femininity. *Hormonal Behavior,* 85: 76-85.

Bleske-Rechek, A., Joseph, W.E., Williquette, H. et al. (2016). *Evolutionary Psychological Science,* 2: 214. doi:10.1007/s40806-016-0056-6.

Browne, T. (1844). *Religio Medici: Its Sequel Christian Morals.* Philadelphia: Lea and Blanchard.

Bulmer, M. (2004). *Francis Galton: Pioneer of Heredity and Biometry.* Baltimore: John Hopkins University Press.

Buss, D. (1989). *The Evolution of Desire.* New York: Basic Books.

Caccone, A. & Powell, J. (1989). Evolutionary divergence among hominids. *Evolution,* 43: 925-942.

Carre, J. & McCormick, C. (2008). In your face: facial metrics predict aggressive behaviour in the laboratory and in varsity and professional hockey players. *Proceedings of the Royal Society, B:* DOI: 10.1098/rspb.2008.0873

Cash, T. & Cash, D. (1982). Women's use of cosmetics: psychosocial correlates and consequences. *International Journal of Cosmetic Science,* 4: 1-14.

Cervera, S., Lahortiqa, F. Martinez-Gonzalez, M. et al. (2003). Neuroticism and low self-esteem as risk factors for incident eating disorders in a prospective cohort study. *International Journal of Eating Disorders,* 33: 271-280.

Chang, C., (2002). *Androgen and androgen receptors: Mechanisms, functions, and clinical applications.* London: Springer.

Cochran, G. & Harpending, H. (2009). *The 10,000 Year Explosion: How Civilization Accelerated Human Evolution.* New York: Basic Books.

Coetzee, V., Greef, J., Stephen, I., Perrett, D. (2014). Cross-Cultural Agreement in Facial Attractiveness Preferences: The Role of Ethnicity and Gender. *PLOS ONE,* DOI: 10.1371/journal.pone.0099629

Cole, T.J. (2003). The secular trend in human physical growth: a biological view. *Economics and Human Biology*, 1:161-168.

Conard, M. A. (2006). Aptitude is Not Enough: How Personality and Behavior Predict Academic Performance. *Journal of Research in Personality,* 40: 339-346.

Corballis, M. (2003). From mouth to hand: Gesture, speech, and the evolution of right-handedness. *Behavioral and Brain Sciences,* 26: 199-208.

Darnall, D. (2013). Mild cases of parental alienation. In Lorandos, D., Bernet, W. & Sauber, S. (Eds). *Parental Alienation: The Handbook for Mental Health and Legal Professionals.* Springfield, IL: Charles C. Thomas Publishers.

Davies, D. (2002). *Anthropology and Theology.* Oxford: Berg.

Davies, S. (2012). *The Artful Species: Aesthetics, Art and Evolution.* Oxford: Oxford University Press.

Dawson, M., Soulieres, I., Gernbacher, M., Mottron, L. (2007). The level and nature of autistic intelligence. *Psychological Science,* 18: 657-662.

De Giustino, D. (2016). *Conquest of Mind: Phrenology and Victorian Social Thought.* London: Routledge.

Deary, I., Yang, J. Davies, G. et al. (2012). Genetic contributions to stability and change in intelligence from childhood to old age. *Nature*, 482: 72-84.

Dixson, B. & Vasey, P. (2012). Beards augment perceptions of men's age, social status, and aggressiveness, but not attractiveness. *Behavioral Ecology,* 23: 481-490.

Dragovic, M., & Hammond, G. (2005). Handedness in schizophrenia: a quantitative review of evidence. *Acta Psychiatrica Scandinavica, 111,* 410–419.

Duckitt, J., Wagner, C., Du Plessis, I. & Birum, I. (2002). The psychological bases of ideology and prejudice: Testing a dual process model. *Journal of Personality and Social Psychology,* 83: 75-93.

Dunkel, C. S., Nedelec, J. L., van der Linden, D., & Marshall, R. L. (2017). Physical Attractiveness and the General Factor of Personality. *Adaptive Human Behavior and Physiology,* 3: 185-197.

Dunkel, C., Nedelec, J., Van der Linden, D. & Marshall, R. (2016). Physical attractiveness and the general factor of personality. *Adaptive Human Behavior and Psychology,* DOI: 10.1007/s40750-016-0055-7

Dunkel, C., Reeve, C., Woodley of Menie, M.A., & Van der Linden, D. (2015). A comparative study of the general factor of personality in Jewish and non-Jewish populations. *Personality and Individual Differences,* 78, 63-67.

Dutton, E., Madison, G. & Dunkel, C. (2017). The Mutant Says in His Heart, "There Is No God": The Rejection of Collective Religiosity Centred Around the Worship of Moral Gods is Associated with High Mutational Load. *Evolutionary Psychological Science,* https://doi.org/10.1007/s40806-017-0133-5

Dutton, E. & Van der Linden, D. (2017). Why is Intelligence Negatively Associated with Religiousness? *Evolutionary Psychological Science,* https://doi.org/10.1007/s40806-017-0101-0

Dutton, E., Van der Linden, D. & Lynn, R. (2016). Population differences in androgen levels: A test of the Differential K Theory. *Personality and Individual Differences,* 90: 289-295.

Dutton, E. & Charlton, B. (2015). *The Genius Famine: Why We Need Geniuses, Why They're Dying Out and Why We Must rescue Them.* Buckingham: University of Buckingham Press.

Dutton, E. & Lynn, R. (2015). *Race and Sport: Evolution and Racial Differences in Sporting Ability.* London: Ulster Institute for Social Research.

Dutton, E. (2010). Latent Social Class Terms and Consumer Culture in Finland: *'Porvari,' 'Amis,'* and *'Pummi'.* *Arctic Anthropology,* 48:1.

Dutton, E. (2008). *Meeting Jesus at University: Rites of Passage and Student Evangelicals.* Aldershot: Ashgate.

Dutton, E. (2007). Eye-glazing and the anthropology of religion: the positive and negative aspects of experiencing and not understanding an emotional phenomenon in religious studies research. *Anthropology Matters,* 9: 1.

Engel, J. (2005). *Epilepsy: Global Issues for the Practicing Neurologist.* New York: Demos Medical Publishing.

Eysenck, H. (1993). Creativity and personality: Suggestions for a theory. *Psychological Inquiry*, 4, 147-178.

Eysenck, H. (1997). *Rebel With a Cause: The Autobiography of Hans Eysenck. Revised Expanded Edition.* New Brunswick: Transaction Publishers.

Fodor, J. (1983). *The Modularity of the Mind: An Essay on Faculty Psychology.* Cambridge, MA: MIT Press.

Furnham, A. & Swami, V. (2007). Perception of female buttocks and breast size in profile. *Social Behavior and Personality*, 35:1-8

Galton, F. (1878). Composite Portraits, *Nature,* (23rd May).

Gangestad, S.W., Yeo, R.A., Shaw, P., Thoma, R., Daniel, W.F., & Korthank, A. (1996). Human leukocyte antigens and hand preference: preliminary observations. *Neuropsychology, 10,* 423-428.

Geschwind, N., & Behan, E. (1982). Left-handedness: associations with immune disease, migraine, and developmental learning disorders. *Proceedings of the National Academy of Science, 79,* 5097-5100.

Gomez, A. (2012). *EMDR Therapy and Adjunct Approaches with Children: Complex Trauma, Attachment, and Dissociation.* New York: Springer Publishing.

Goodman, J. (2014). The wages of sinistrality: handedness, brain structure, and human capital accumulation. *Journal of Economic Perspectives, 28,* 193-212.

Goodwyn, E. (2012). *The Neurobiology of the Gods: How Brain Physiology Shapes the Recurrent Imagery of Myth and Dreams.* London: Routledge.

Granacher, B. (2007). *Traumatic Brain Injury: Methods for Clinical and Forensic Neuropsychiatric Assessment, Second Edition.* CRC Press.

Gueguen, N. (2013). Effects of a Tattoo on Men's Behavior and Attitudes Toward Women: An Experimental Field Study. *Archives of Sexual Behavior*, 42:1517.

Hallissy, M. (1995). *A Companion to Chaucer's Canterbury Tales.* Greenwood Publishing.

Halpern, D.F., Haviland , M.G., & Killian, C.D. (1998). Handedness and sex differences in intelligence: Evidence from the Medical College Admission Test. *Brain & Cognition, 38,* 87–101.

Hamilton J. B., (1958). Age, sex and genetic factors in the regulation of hair growth in man. A comparison of Caucasian and Japanese populations. In: Montagna W, Ellis RA, eds, *The biology of hair growth*. New York: Academic Press, 399–433.

Hamilton, W. & Zuk, M. (1982). Heritable True Fitness and Bright Birds: A Role for Parasites? *Science,* 218:

Harmon, L. R. (1961). The High School Background of Science Doctorates: A Survey Reveals the Influence of Class Size, Region of Origin, as Well as Ability, in PhD Production. *Science* 133: 679–688.

Hatton, T. (2013). How have Europeans grown so tall? *Oxford Economic Papers,* 66: 349-372.

Havlíček, J., Třebický, V., Valentova, J.V. et al. (2016). Men's preferences for women's breast size and shape in four cultures. *Evolution & Human Behavior*.

Hayward, K. & Yar, M. (2006). The Chav phenomenon: Consumption, media, and the construction of a new underclass. *Crime, Media and Culture,* 2: 9-28.

Hecht, D. (2010). Depression and the hyperactive right-hemisphere. *Neuroscientific Research*, 68: 77–87.

Helgasson, A., Palsson, S., Gudbjartsson, D. et al. (2008). An association between the kinship and fertility of human couples. *Science,* 319: 813-816.

Herrnstein, R. & Murray, C. (1994). *The Bell Curve: Intelligence and Class Structure in American Life*. New York: Free Press.

Heywood, W., Patrick, K., Smith, A. et al. (2012). Who Gets Tattoos? Demographic and Behavioral Correlates of Ever Being Tattooed in a Representative Sample of Men and Women. *Annals of Epidemiology,* 22: 51-56.

Highfield, R., Wiseman, R. & Jenkins, R. (2009). How your looks betray your personality. *New Scientist,* (11 February).

Hindley, S. W., & Damon, A., (1973). Some genetic traits in Solomon Island populations IV.
Mid-palangeal hair. *American Journal of Physical Anthropology, 39,* 191-194.

Hines, M. (2011). Prenatal endocrine influences on sexual orientation and on sexually differentiated childhood behaviour. *Frontiers in Neuroendocrinology,* 32: 170-182.

Irwing, P. (2013). Sex differences in *g*: An analysis of the US standardization sample of the WAIS III. In Nyborg, H. (Ed). *Race and Sex Differences in Intelligence and Personality: A Tribute to Richard Lynn at 80.* London: Ulster Institute for Social Research.

Janowsky, J., Oviatt, S., Orwoll, E. (1994). Testosterone influences spatial cognition in older men. *Behavioral Neuroscience,* 108: 325–32.

Jensen, A. (1998). *The g Factor: The Science of the Mind.* Newport: Praeger.

Johnston, D.W., Nicholls, M.E.R., Shah, M., & Shields, M.A. (2013). Handedness, health and cognitive development: evidence from children in the National Longitudinal Survey of Youth. *Journal of the Royal Statistical Society A, 176,* 841-860.

Joiner, M. & Kogel, A. (Eds). (2016). *Basic Clinical Radiobiology.* CRC Press.

Kanazawa, S. (2014). Intelligence and obesity: Which way does the direction of causation go? *Current Opinion,* 321-344.

Kanazawa, S. (2012). *The Intelligence Paradox: Why the Intelligent Choice Isn't Always the Smart One.* Hoboken: John Wiley & Sons.

Kanazawa, S. (2011). Intelligence and physical attractiveness. *Intelligence,* 39: 7-14.

Kaufman, S., DeYoung, C., Reiss, D. & Gray, J. (2011). General intelligence predicts reasoning ability for evolutionarily familiar content. *Intelligence,* 39: 311-322.

Kirasic, K. (1989). Acquisition and utilization of spatial information by elderly adults: implications for day to day situations. In L. Poon, D. Rubin & B. Wilson. (Eds). *Everyday Cognition in Adulthood and Later Life.* Cambridge: Cambridge University Press.

Kolipakam, M. & Kalish, R. (2007). Male-pattern baldness. In *Diseases and Disoders, Vol. II.* New York: Marshall Cavendish.

Kosinski, M. & Wang, Y. (2017). Deep neural networks are more accurate than humans at detecting sexual orientation from facial images. *OSF, https://osf.io/zn79k/*

Kretschmer, E. (1931). *Physique and Character.* London: Routledge.

Kleisner, K., Chvátalová, V. & Flegr, J. (2014). Perceived intelligence is associated with measured intelligence in men but not women. *PLoS ONE* 9: e81237. https://doi.org/10.1371/journal.pone.0081237

Koenig, H., McGue, M., Krueger, R. & Bouchard, T. (2005). Genetic and environmental influences on religiousness: Findings for retrospective and current religiousness ratings. *Journal of Personality.* 73: 471-478.

Lavater, J. (1826). *Physiognomy.* Cowie, Low & Co.

Laythe, B., Finkel, D. & Kirkpatrick, L. (2001). Predicting prejudice from religious fundamentalism and right wing authoritarianism: A multiple regression analysis. *Journal for the Scientific Study of Religion,* 40: 1-10.

Lee, A., Hibbs, C., Wright, M. et al. (2017). Assessing the accuracy of perceptions of intelligence based on heritable facial features. *Intelligence,* 64: 1-8.

Lewis, D., Conroy-Beam, D., Al-Shawaf, L. et al. (2011). Friends with Benefits: The evolved psychology of same- and opposite-sex friendship. *Evolutionary Psychology,* doi/full/10.1177/147470491100900407

Lewis, K. & Bear, B. (2008). *Manual of School Health - E-Book: A Handbook for School Nurses, Educators, and Health Professionals.* Amsterdam: Elsevier.

Lewis, M. (2012). A Facial Attractiveness Account of Gender Asymmetries in Interracial Marriage. *PLOS ONE,* 7: 2.

Liem, E., Joiner, T., Tsueda, K. & Sessler, D. (2005). Increased Sensitivity to Thermal Pain and Reduced Subcutaneous Lidocaine Efficacy in Redheads. *Anesthesiology,* 10: 509-514.

Liem, E., Lin, C., Suleman, M. et al. (2004). Anesthetic Requirement is Increased in Redheads. *Anesthesiology,* 101: 279-83.

Lippa. E. (2005). Sexual orientation and personality. *Annual Review of Sex Research,* 16. 119-153.

Little, A., Jones, B. & DeBruine, L. (2011). Facial attractiveness: evolutionary based research. *Philosophical Transactions, B.* 366: 1638–1659.

Little, A. & Perrett, D. (2007). Using composite images to assess accuracy in personality attribution to faces. *British Journal of Psychology,* 98: 111-126.

Lynn, C. & Madeiros, C. (2017). Tattooing commitment, quality and football in Southeastern North America. In Lynn, C. et al. (Eds). *Evolution Education in the American South: Culture, Politics, and Resources in and around Alabama.* New York: Palgrave Macmillan.

Lynn, R. (2011). *Dysgenics: Genetic Deterioration in Modern Populations. 2nd Edition.* London: Ulster Institute for Social Research.

Långström N, Rahman, Q., Carlström, E. & Lichtenstein, P. (2010). Genetic and environmental effects on same-sex sexual behavior: a population study of twins in Sweden. *Archives of Sexual Behavior,* 39: 75–80

Madison, G. & Ullén, F. (2012). Statistical learning and prejudice. *Behavioral and Brain Sciences,* 35: 30-31.

Malick, F., Haward, J. & Koo. J. (2008). Understanding the psychology of the cosmetic patients. *Dermatologic Therapy,* 21: 47-53.

Manning, J. T., Bundred, P. E., Newton, D. J., & Flanagan, B. F. (2003). The second to fourth digit ratio and variation in the androgen receptor gene. *Evolution and Human Behavior, 24,* 399-405.

Markow, T.A. (1992). Human handedness and the concept of developmental stability. *Genetica, 87,* 87-94.

Marks, J.S., & Williamson, D.F. (1991). Left-handedness and life expectancy. *New England Journal of Medicine, 325,* 1042.

Mazur, A., & Booth, A. (1998). Testosterone and dominance in men. *Behavioral and Brain Sciences, 21,* 353-363.

McKenzie, J., Taghavi-Khonsary, M. & Tindell, G. (2000). Neuroticism and academic achievement: the Furneaux Factor as a measure of academic rigor. *Personality and Individual Differences,* 29: 3-11.

Miller, G. (2000). *The Mating Mind: How Sexual Choice Shaped the Evolution of Human Nature.* New York: Anchor Books.

Nettle, D. (2007). *Personality: What Makes You Who You Are.* Oxford: Oxford University Press.

Nickman, S., Rosenfeld, A., Fine, P. et al. (2005). Children in adoptive families: Overview and update. *Journal of the American Association of Child and Adolescent Psychiatry,* 44: 987-995.

Nieschlag, E. & Behre, H. (2013). Testosterone Therapy. In Nieschlag, E. & Behre, H. (Eds). *Andrology: Male Reproductive Health and Dysfunction.* New York: Springer.

Nijhout, H.F., & Davidowitz, G. (2003). Developmental perspectives on phenotypic variation, canalization, and fluctuating asymmetry. In M. Polak (Ed.), *Developmental instability: Causes and consequences.* (pp. 3-13). New York: Oxford University Press.

Nicholls, M.E.R., Chapman, H.L., Loetscher, T., & Grimshaw, G.M. (2010). The relationship between hand preference, hand performance, and general cognitive ability. *Journal of the International Neuropsychological Society, 16*, 585-592.

Nowosielski, K. et al. (2012). Tattoos, Piercing, and Sexual Behaviors in Young Adults. *Journal of Sexual Medicine*, 9:2307.

Oosterhof, N. & Todorov, A. (2008). The functional basis of face evaluation. *PNAS,* 105: 11087–11092.

Parentini, L. (1995). *The Joy of Healthy Skin: A Lifetime Guide to Beautiful, Problem-free Skin.* Prentice-Hall.

Passini, F. & Warren, N. (1966). A universal conception of personality structure? *Journal of Personality and Social Psychology,* 4: 44-49.

Percival, M. & Tytler, G. (Eds.), (2005). *Physiognomy in Profile: Lavater's Impact on European Culture.* Newark: University of Delaware Press.

Peterson, R. & Palmer, C. (2017). The Effects of Physical Attractiveness on Political Beliefs. *Politics and the Life Sciences,* 36: 3-16.

Pincott, J. (16th April 2011). Why are redheads more sensitive? *Psychology Today,* https://www.psychologytoday.com/blog/love-sex-and-babies/201104/why-are-redheads-more-sensitive

Porter, M. (2005). *Windows of the Soul: Physiognomy in European Culture 1470-1780.* Oxford: Clarendon Press.

Rahman, Q., Sharp, J., McVeigh, M. & Ho, M.-L. (2017). Sexual Orientation-Related Differences in Virtual Spatial Navigation and Spatial Search Strategies. *Archives of Sexual Behavior,* 46: 1279-1294.

Rahman Q, Symeonides D. & Symeonides, D. (2007). Neurodevelopmental Correlates of Paraphilic Sexual Interests in Men. *Archives of Sexual Behavior*, 37 166–172.

Reed, J. & Blunk, E. (1990). The influence of facial hair on impression formation. *Social Behavior and Personality,* 18: 169-175.

Resnick, S., Berenbaum, S., Gottesman, I. et al. (1986). Early hormonal influences on cognitive functioning in congenital adrenal hyperplasia. *Developmental Psychology*, 22: 191–198.

Robb, A. (5th February 2014). Want to look older and more aggressive? Grow a beard. *New Republic,* https://newrepublic.com/article/116472/psychologists-bearded-men-look-older-more-aggressive-higher-status

Ross, C. (1974). *Edward IV.* Los Angeles: University of California Press.

RT. (10th May 2017). Scientific racism? Chinese professor defends facial-recognition study after Google scoffing. https://www.rt.com/news/387849-study-faces-criminals-china/

Rule, N., Garrett, J. & Abady, N. (2010). On the perception of religious group membership from faces. PLoS ONE, 5(12):e14241. doi: 10.1371/journal.pone.0014241.

Rushton, J. P. & Templer, D. (2012). Do pigmentation and the melanocortin system modulate aggression and sexuality in humans as they do in other animals? *Personality and Individual Differences,* 53: 4-8.

Rushton, J. & Davison Ankney, C. (2009). Whole Brain Size and General Mental Ability: A Review. *International Journal of Neuroscience,* 119: 692-732.

Rushton, J. P. & Irwing, P. (2008). A General Factor of Personality from two meta-analyses of the Big Five. *Personality and Individual Differences,* 45: 679-683.

Rushton, J. P. (2005). Ethnic nationalism, Evolutionary Psychology and Genetic Similarity Theory. Nations and Nationalism, 11: 489-507.

Rushton, J. P. (2000). *Race, Evolution and Behavior: A Life History Perspective. Third Edition.* Charles Darwin Institute.

Salter, F. (2007). *On Genetic Interests: Family, Ethnicity and Humanity in an Age of Mass Migration.* New Brunswick, NJ: Transaction Publishers.

Semlyn, J., King, M., Varney, J. & Hagger-Johnson, G. (2016). Sexual orientation and symptoms of common mental disorder or low wellbeing: combined meta-analysis of 12 UK population health surveys. *BMC Psychiatry,* 16: 67.

Sheldon, W. (1940). *The Varieties of Human Physique.* New York: Harper and Brothers.

Silventoinen, K., Posthuma, D., van Beijsterveldt, M. et al. (2006). Genetic contributions to the association between height and intelligence: evidence from Dutch twin data from childhood to middle age. *Genes, Brain and Behaviour,* 5: 585-595.

Simmel, G. (1957). Fashion. *American Journal of Sociology, 62,* 541-558.

Sprague-McRae, J., Rosenblum, R. & Morrison, L. (2014). *Child Neurology Encounter Guides: A Comprehensive Clinician Toolkit for Guiding Child Neurology Encounters.* Indianapolis: Dog Ear Publishing.

Soper, H., Satz, R., Orsini, D., Henry, R., Zvi, J.C., & Schulman, M. (1986). Handedness patterns in autism suggests subtypes. *Journal of Autism and Developmental Disorders, 16*, 155-167.

Soto, C., John, O., Gosling, S. & Potter, J. (2011). Age differences in personality traits from 10 to 65: Big Five domains and facets in a large cross-sectional sample. *Journal of Personality and Social Psychology,* 100: 330-348.

Steiner, I. (1980). Attribution of choice. In Fishbein, M. (Ed). *Progress in Social Psychology, Volume I.* Psychology Press.

Swami, V., Tran, U., Brooks, L. et al. (2013). Body image and personality: associations between the Big Five Personality Factors, actual-ideal weight discrepancy, and body appreciation. *Scandinavian Journal of Psychology,* 54: 146-151.

Swami, V., Pietschnig, J., Bertl, B. & Voracek, M. (2012). Personality differences between tattooed and non-tattooed individuals. *Psychological Reports,* 111: 97-106.

Swift-Gallant, A., Coome, L., Ashley-Monks, D. & VanderLaan, D. (2017). Handedness is a biomarker of variation in anal sex role behavior and Recalled Childhood Gender Nonconformity among gay men. *PLOS ONE:* https://doi.org/10.1371/journal.pone.0170241

Tate, J. & Shelton, B. (2008). Personality correlates of tattooing and body piercing in a college sample: The kids are alright. *Personality and Individual Differences,* 45: 281-285.

Thorburn, D. (2004). *How to Spot Hidden Alcoholics: Using Behavioral Clues to Recognize Addiction in Its Early Stages.* Northridge, CA: Galt Publishing.

Thornhill, R. & Gangestad, S. (2008). *The Evolutionary Biology of Human Female Sexuality.* Oxford: Oxford University Press.

Tsukahara, J., Harrison, T. & Engle, R. (2016). The relationship between baseline pupil size and intelligence. *Cognitive Psychology,* 91: 109-123.

Van der Linden, D., Dunkel, C. & Petrides, K. (2016). The General Factor of Personality (GFP) as Social Effectiveness: A Literature review. *Personality and Individual Differences,* 101: 98-105.

Varcarolis, E. (2014). *Essentials of Psychiatric Mental Health Nursing.* Amsterdam: Elsevier Health Sciences.

Verma, A. & Verma, A. (2015). A Novel Review of the Evidence Linking Myopia and High Intelligence. *Journal of Opthalmology,* 271746.

Vernon, P., J. Wickett, G. Bazana, & R. Stelmack. (2000). The Neuro-psychology and Psychophysiology of Human Intelligence. In R. Sternberg, (ed.). *Handbook of Intelligence.* Cambridge: Cambridge University Press.

Weinbauer, G., Gromoll, J., Simoni, M. & Nieschlag, E. (2013). Physiology of testicular function. In Nischlag, E. & Behre, H. (Eds.). *Andrology: Male Reproductive Health and Dysfunction.* New York: Springer.

Weisberg, Y. J., DeYoung, C. G., & Hirsh, J. B. (2011). Gender differences in personality across the ten aspects of the Big Five. *Frontiers in Psychology, 2:* 178.

West, P. & Packer, C. (2002). Sexual selection, temperature and the lion's mane. *Science,* 297: 1339-1343.

Westlund, N., Oinonen, K. A., Mazmanian, D., & Bird, J. L. (2015). The value of middle phalangeal hair as an anthropometric marker: A review of the literature. *HOMO,* 66: 316-331.

What Happens in Sunny Beach . . . , Series 1, Episode 1. Channel 4. 9th January 2014.

Wiggins, J., Wiggins, N. & Conger, J. (1968). Correlates of heterosexual somatic preference. *Journal of Personality and Social Psychology,* 10: 82-89.

Wilde, O. (2012). *The Picture of Dorian Gray.* London: The Folio Society.

Willis, J. & Todorov, A. (2006). First Impressions: Making Up Your Mind After a 100-Ms Exposure to a Face. *Psychological Science,* 17: doi/10.1111/j.1467-9280.2006.01750.x

Winston, R. (2010). *Bad Ideas? An Arresting History of Our Inventions.* London: Transworld Publishers.

Woodley of Menie, M.A., Saraff, M., Pestow, R. & Fernandes, H. (2017). Social Epistasis Amplifies the Fitness Costs of Deleterious Mutations, Engendering Rapid Fitness Decline Among Modernized Populations. *Evolutionary Psychological Science,* 17: 181-191.

Woodley of Menie, M.A. & Fernandes, H. (2016). The secular decline in general intelligence from decreasing developmental stability: Theoretical and empirical considerations. *Personality and Individual Differences,* 92: 194-199.

Wu, X. & Zhang, X. (2016). Automated Inference on Criminality using Face Images. arXiv:1611.04135.

Zahavi, A. & Zahavi, A. (1997). *The Handicap Principle: The Missing Piece of Darwin's Puzzle.* Oxford: Oxford University Press.

Made in the USA
Monee, IL
01 September 2020